The Illustrated Cavalry Versus Infantry

The Illustrated
Cavalry Versus Infantry

An Evaluation of the Practices of the Armies of
the 18th & 19th Centuries from the Perspective
of the Early 20th Century

F. N. Maude

LEONAUR

The Illustrated Cavalry Versus Infantry
An Evaluation of the Practices of the Armies of the 18th & 19th Centuries from the
Perspective of the Early 20th Century
by F. N. Maude

First published under the title
Cavalry Versus Infantry

Leonaur is an imprint of Oakpast Ltd

Copyright in this form © 2013 Oakpast Ltd

ISBN: 978-1-78282-148-9 (hardcover)
ISBN: 978-1-78282-149-6 (softcover)

http://www.leonaur.com

Publisher's Notes

The views expressed in this book are not necessarily
those of the publisher.

Contents

Original Editor's Preface

Captain Maude is so well known to military readers that no further introduction seems necessary. It is sufficient to say that the essays here presented were originally published in the *Civil and Military Gazette*, of Lahore, India, and that their military value and interest are such that they are deemed well worth preservation in book form. The views expressed by Captain Maude are original and fearless; and whether accepted in their entirety by the reader or not, they cannot be perused without benefit by any thinking soldier.

U. S. Infantry and Cavalry School,
December 1, 1896.

Cavalry Versus Infantry in the Napoleonic Era

Were it not that for the last century, (19th), and more we in England have always sinned against the axiom that the tactics of an army should be based on the racial characteristics of the men who compose it, I should apologize for referring to the old truism again. Unfortunately for us, the record of our tactical literature, with few exceptions, and of our drill regulations and instructions for umpires, with even fewer, show that the axiom has never been applied to our own case. Therefore it seems opportune to call attention to how the great heresy, that cavalry cannot charge unshaken infantry, first arose amongst us; for unquestionably had it not been an already accepted one with our generals and staff, even before the introduction of the breechloader, that the usefulness of cavalry on the battlefield was a thing of the past, the cavalry would not so tacitly have accepted their position as has actually been the case.

The origin of the doctrine is briefly this. At the close of the great Napoleonic struggle it had become an accepted article of faith, notably in the French Army, but pretty generally also in all continental cavalries, that horses could not be got to face the bayonets of a square, let alone its fire. And we, being almost entirely destitute of a military literature of our own, accepted this dictum tacitly, without stopping to enquire whether our own cavalry had experienced this difficulty with their mounts or not.

What little tactical literature we possessed, which we owed almost entirely to the pens of infantry officers, bore out this idea pretty fully, for the record of our infantry against French cavalry was so high, though not quite as high as these authors would have had us believe, that there was at least some justification for the idea, provided always that infantry were infantry and cavalry cavalry all the world over, no matter from what nation they originally were raised—a premise which I entirely decline to accept If, therefore, it can be shown, as I believe it can, that whatever may have been the case as regards French cavalry against British infantry, it was emphatically not the case with the *rôles* reversed, and if further the reasons why things happened as they did in the former case can be clearly shown, I imagine that a great part of the opposition displayed by modern British umpires and tacticians to the proposed method of employing cavalry masses in battle nowadays will be considerably diminished.

Let us trace the historical development of the subject. At the close of the Seven Years' War[1] the Prussian cavalry were the absolute arbiters of the battlefield, wherever the nature of the ground gave them a fair show. Seydlitz at Rozbach, the Baireuth Dragoons at Hohenfriedberg with their record of 66 stand of colours, 4,000 prisoners, and 5 guns, are known to almost every officer who has passed for his majority—nay, even to every cadet fresh out of Sandhurst. But the exploits of our own regiments in the Low Countries, forty years after, and in the Peninsula, are better known frequently in the ranks than amongst the officers, though the names of the actions are all there on the regimental plate and on their standards, where they have them for all to read.

How many officers, even in the regiments that took part in it, know anything of the action of "*Villiers en Couche*" on the 24th of April, 1793, where two British and two Austrian squadrons broke and dispersed a huge square consisting of six battalions of French infantry, killing and wounding 900 men and capturing 400 more with 5 guns. As my authority, the late Major-General Mitchell, remarks:

"There was no appearance then of the new light that has since broken in upon the horses, and rendered them so conscious of the danger to be apprehended from the fire of musketry as to make them bear their reluctant riders far away from the bayonets of the infantry."

How many more know anything of the Battle of Cateau Cambresis, fought two days later, where an Austrian regiment of *cuirassiers*, together with nine squadrons of British cavalry, rivalled the Prussians at Rozbach by routing and dispersing the infantry and artillery of a French corps 27,000 strong, and destroying some 3,000 of them, besides capturing 22 guns; and later in the day, when a second column of the French was charged by four British and two Austrian squadrons,

---

1. *Frederick the Great & the Seven Years' War* by F. W. Longman, also published by Leonaur.

GENERAL SEYDLITZ

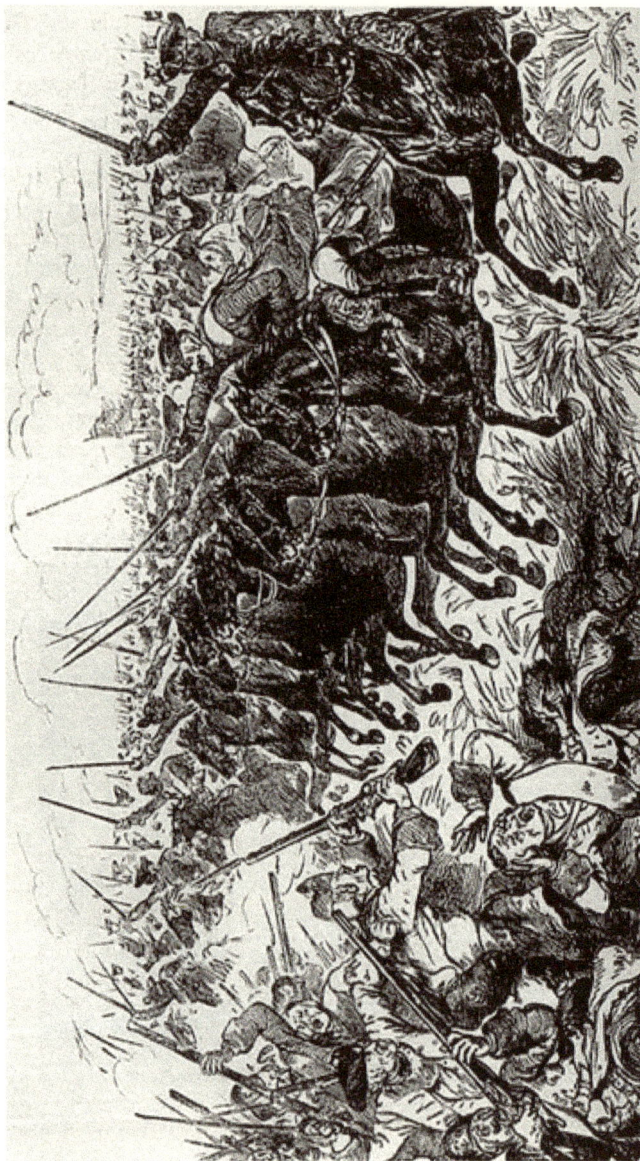

Baireuth Dragoons at the Battle of Hohenfriedberg

and defeated with a loss of 1,000 men and 10 guns. The total loss of the cavalry for the day being 16 officers and 380 men, and that of the enemy 5,000 men and 32 guns. And these charges, too, it must be remembered, were delivered against infantry equal in armament, but most decidedly superior in morale, to anything, in the way of infantry the French succeeded in putting into the field between 1809 and 1814.

The Peninsula War furnishes altogether eight examples of British cavalry charging French infantry, not counting skirmishes; and out of these eight charges, five were successful, two failures, attributable to the nature of the ground, and one undisguised or unaccounted-for disaster. I have no space to give them all in detail, but will take one simple instance as showing the power which our cavalry possessed even under the most unfavourable circumstances. It is the third charge in the day of Salamanca, Le Marchant's Heavy Brigade against steady French infantry, and is quoted from the account of a warm partisan of the infantry, who wrote under the signature of A. Z. shortly after the events:

> The nature of the ground, which was an open wood of evergreen oaks, and which grew more obstructed as the cavalry advanced, had caused the men of the three regiments to become a *good, deal mixed in each other's ranks*; and the front being at the same time constantly changing as the right was brought forward, the whole had now crowded into a solid line without any intervals. In this order, but without any confusion, they pressed rapidly forward upon another French brigade, which, taking advantage of the trees, had formed a '*colonne serrée*' and stood awaiting the charge. These men reserved their fire with much coolness till the cavalry came within twenty yards, when they poured it in with a deadly and tremendous effect upon the concentrated mass of men and horses.
> The gallant Le Marchant and Captain White of his staff were killed, Colonel Elley was wounded, and *it is thought* that nearly one-third of the dragoons came to the ground; but as the remainder maintained sufficient command of their horses to dash forward, they succeeded in breaking the French ranks and dispersing them in utter confusion over the field.

The writer's object is to prove the invulnerability of an infantry square. To my mind he proves the exact opposite, for he admits that they were cool and tried soldiers who took every advantage of the ground, and who were in even a better formation, as regards volume of fire on a given front, than they would have been in ordinary square; and yet they were powerless to stop the rush of cavalry blown and disorganised by previous fighting and sadly hampered by the ground: and all this even if the one-third brought to the ground is admitted.

Unfortunately for A. Z., the losses of the regiments, as officially sent in, do not tally with his assertion, for in the whole day's fighting the brigade only lost 4 officers, 94 men, and 140 horses killed and wounded, of whom only 23 men and 68 horses belonged to the first category, and the strength of the brigade could not have been much less on the morning of the action than 1,000 sabres.

Now, almost at the same period, what were the French cavalry doing? They had actually fallen so low that it was an accepted axiom with the *cuirassiers*—the pick of the army—to charge only at a trot, and when they exceeded that pace it was only because the horses took the law into their own hands and fairly ran away, sometimes towards the enemy, sometimes in a contrary direction. Considerable doubt has been thrown on this statement of late years in England, but I think it can be shown to be an incontestable fact. Not only have we Jomini's[2] statement that it was the case, but here is the description of the charge of the *cuirassiers* at Eckmühl, from the pen of a Würtemberg cavalry colonel, Graf von Bismarck, who rode alongside them in this attack, with his own regiment:

> Meanwhile the *cuirassier* divisions had followed at a trot, and met the attack of the Austrian Reserve cavalry in so brilliant a fashion that the infantry of Lannes' corps halted to cheer them . . . . The *cuirassiers* laid special stress on riding boot to boot, and never moved at a faster pace than the trot. One heard constantly from their ranks the officers speaking to their men, not commanding, '*Serrez, Cuirassiers, serrez*.' Just before closing with the enemy, the generals and colonels again repeated the command—'*En avant. Marche, marche!*' which was repeated by all the men, but the pace was never increased. This '*en avant*' was only the French equivalent of the Russian '*Hurrah!*'

Von Bismarck, whose work on cavalry tactics was translated into English by Captain Beamish of the King's German Legion which, by

2. *The Campaign of Waterloo, 1815 - A Political & Military History from the French Perspective* by Antoine Henri Jomini, also published by Leonaur.

Cᴜɪʀᴀssɪᴇʀ 1809

BATTLE OF ECKMÜHL

the way, is about the best book on cavalry in the English language prior to the date of about 1875 and is to be found in the Library of the United Service Institution at Simla, from whose shelves it appears to have been only twice removed since it came there), and who, though a German, was a warm admirer of many French things and had fought by their side for many years, quotes this example not in the least as a point to be avoided, but otherwise—so far had the Germans fallen from the traditions of Frederick the Great.

But worse was still to come. General Mitchell quotes some characteristic exploits (?) of the French cavalry in 1813, from which I borrow the following somewhat condensed instances of the combat of irregular horse against these same famed *cuirassiers* of Napoleon, which deserve to be framed, glazed, and hung up in every barrack-room as examples of the way how not to do things. Here is the first:

> While we (the Don Cossacks) were yet engaged in driving back the advanced parties, a mass of cavalry, greatly exceeding us in number, advanced in haste from the town, and drew up in our front; they were formed in 'column of squadrons,' and as the skirmishers fell back, we soon had nothing but this heavy mass in front of us. Though the Cossacks could gain little in a contest with so large a force, it was equally evident that still less was to be risked in assailing them; so that, urged on, partly by their natural instinct, and partly by command, they pushed forward to the attack.
>
> The French advanced at a short trot to meet us, and under the apprehension, probably, that the Russians would attempt to dash into the intervals between the squadrons, these were closed up to quarter distance. Thus formed, they bore directly on the centre of our line, which instantly opened out, the Cossacks throwing themselves on the flank and rear of the hostile columns; and the French, finding no enemy to contend with in front, soon halted, whilst the warriors of the *Don* kept firing into the mass or spearing the flank files.
>
> The French had by this time got into such complete confusion that they could undertake no evolution of any kind, and the Cossacks, on their side totally unable to move in compact order, never thought of dispersing by a bold onset the helpless mob they were assailing. The flank files of the French having faced outwards, and their rear files having gone to the right about,

the whole party sprung their carbines, and a regular, if not very destructive, fusillade ensued, which lasted for half an hour. At the end of that time the heads of some infantry columns, accompanied by artillery, were seen advancing, and the first shots from the latter released the French from their unpleasant predicament; the whole swarm of Cossacks vanishing.

It was perfectly evident that a want of skill in manoeuvring, and a total ignorance of the real nature of cavalry action, had induced the French to crowd together into column. One-third of their number, well and bravely led, would have driven the three regiments of Cossacks from the field with perfect ease. This action also gave proofs of the utter unfitness of the Cossacks for anything like a home charge, as well as of the little that can be effected by their loose and irregular mode of fighting.

Here is another example, which occurred about a month later, even more instructive, as showing how much the French relied on their *mounted fire*:

While the Cossacks were forming up, the French also completed their movement; their entire body, except a feeble reserve behind, '*en muraille*' in a single line without intervals. The Cossacks threw themselves upon the unwieldy mass, and were received by a sharp fire from the enemy's carbines; the French had not even drawn their sabres. The Russians at first gave way before this fire; and whilst they were again forming for a second onset, a movement was observed in the enemy's lines. I expected that we were to be attacked; but I was mistaken, for the French only wheeled outwards with a view to gain ground for the necessary intervals between their squadrons, and having effected this, they again wheeled up.

The object of this change of formation was, I suppose, to prevent their flanks from being turned, a mode of attack the Cossacks adopt instinctively on all occasions. The Cossacks were pretty sharply told not to shrink from the fire of the carbines, and officers rode behind the line with orders to cut down the first man who should fall back. Several squadrons were also appointed to turn the enemy during the front attack.

These orders were punctually obeyed. The Cossacks pressed in upon the French and surrounded their squadrons; and I had here an opportunity of seeing several of the enormous dragoons, who had fired their carbines at us, cut down or speared before they could put sword in hand. At first the French defended themselves as well as men could do when contending at a halt against active, moving enemies; but some of the squadrons having turned, the rest gradually followed their example. The reserve also, instead of advancing to support the front line, only joined the flight, so that in a short time the entire plain was covered with scattered horsemen. Not a single half-squadron was to be seen together; it was a complete chase, during which most of those who were afterwards taken fell from their horses. The defeat of the French on this occasion was entirely owing to their inability to move, and to the want of confidence in their own prowess naturally resulting from such a deficiency.

One other instance deserves to be quoted as showing how cavalry that could move dealt with the Cossacks. It is still the same eyewitness speaking:

As we approached some hillocks, and while very carelessly driving the French before us, a regiment of *chasseurs* that had been concealed by the ground suddenly made their appearance. Fortunately for us, they attacked only at a trot and in column of squadrons, so that we easily evaded their onset. The officer commanding the Cossacks had at the beginning of the action left half his men behind as a reserve—an arrangement which again brought the line to a stand; for, as soon as this second line joined us, the French halted, threw out skirmishers, and, going to the right about, returned at a trot, followed by the whole swarm of Cossacks. We had thus advanced some distance when we perceived another body of their cavalry advancing at a sharp trot against our left; they appeared to be two squadrons of the Hussars of Alsace.

To meet them our commanding officer wheeled up a division and remained with the right and centre fronting the Chasseurs, who had again halted and re-formed. The Hussars then sounded the gallop, and two squadrons, hitherto concealed by the leading squadrons, dashed out to either flank, wheeled into line, and the whole threw themselves at full gallop, *without firing a single shot,* upon us; in two minutes not a Cossack remained on the field.

There are many more interesting examples in General Mitchell's book which my space prevents me from quoting. I can only draw attention to his concluding remarks. He says:

> Let us recollect that the cavalry who, in column and at a trot, attacked such feeble troops (*i.e.*, the Cossacks), and afterwards formed a kind of solid mob, in order to repel them by the fire of their carbines; who drew up in line to contend in regular fusillade with the same foes; who forgot that they had sabres by their sides, and thought only of their spurs when retiring; that these men, who, to say nothing more, *charged at a trot, and fled at a gallop*, were the soldiers of Napoleon, fought perhaps under his very eye, and had certainly been trained according to his regulations; and we can form some sort of idea of the views on cavalry warfare prevalent in the Imperial Army.

These three illustrations refer only to cavalry versus cavalry, but I could give page after page of similar examples of their action against infantry, notably their celebrated charges against our squares at Waterloo; and with this evidence before them, I appeal to all officers of the British Army, whether cavalry or infantry, whether it is right or fair that deductions drawn from the deeds of such troops can be legitimately applied to the descendants of those who rode with Le Marchant at Salamanca, or with Ponsonby and the Union Brigade at Waterloo.

Of course, if it is once admitted that even in the old days of flintlock muskets, infantry were unassailable by cavalry, all prospect for their successful employment in the future falls to the ground; but I submit that, whatever may have been the state of the case as regards French cavalry against British infantry, no case whatever is made out by history when the rules were reversed. In the account of the charge at Salamanca, quoted above, it is distinctly shown that our cavalry, even when broken and disorganised by two previous attacks, and still further hampered by difficult ground and trees, could yet bear down perfectly steady French troops, who retained their courage insufficiently to give their assailants a volley at twenty yards; and it is maintained that no such shattering death-dealing wave of fire can be reasonably expected from any troops likely to be attacked on the battlefield of today, (as at time of first publication).

As modern infantry tactics stand, a square is an almost inconceivable formation; instead of it only long lines of more or less shaken skirmishers are to be met with: and allowing that the point-blank

AUSTRIAN–PRUSSIAN CUIRASSIERS

range of their weapons- is good against the cavalry target for 600 yards, if held horizontal—a condition not often fulfilled, as experience proves—yet even then I doubt whether the fire to be confronted is either physically or morally greater than it formerly was.

Besides, no one ever has proposed to send cavalry against absolutely unshaken infantry direct, and even if they did propose to do so, the conditions of the modern battlefield, with its fire-swept zone 3,000 yards in depth, renders it next door to impossible to find such a target for them. What they have proposed is merely this: that cavalry should on occasion be prepared to charge even what appear to be unshaken Infantry; for, till the experiment has been tried, no one can tell whether they actually are unshaken or not. If they are not shaken, well, there will be no mistake about the result; if they are, equally there will be no mistake, but it will be the infantry who will find out what it means. But to get troops and leaders to risk so much, they must be taught to ride fearlessly, and to have confidence in their own power; but our present umpire training is hardly the way to make them do so.

Short Service and Discipline

The amateur British army-reformer is never happy but when he is digging up the seed of a new reform to see how it is getting on, and is always disappointed when he finds that the tree has not grown in a night.

I agree with him so far, that the system is not doing uniformly well everywhere, but I think these unsatisfactory results are far more due to imperfect comprehension of the nature of treatment it requires, than to any inherent defect in the system itself. Some few regiments, both of horse and foot, I have seen, particularly in India, which to my mind prove conclusively the value of even the imperfect copy of the original we possess; and these have led me to think of what might be accomplished throughout, with a stricter adherence to our own type and a little more loyalty in carrying it out.

The German statistics of losses in battle prove that the German system made soldiers capable of fighting their own weight of Frenchmen; but other evidence goes to show that the German soldiers, though victorious, fell short of our ideal of what soldiers should be. Against this, which might be taken to justify condemnation of short service in principle, we must take into consideration what the true limits of this short service was and is, and what was the nature of the men, and the previous training of the officers, before comparing it with our own. Taking the infantry only, the length of their service with the colours was but two years and nine months against our seven years; and in that time the company officers, themselves with only seven weeks' war service, and not all with even that, had to make out of (next to the Russian) perhaps the most peace-loving race in Europe soldiers capable of standing up in fair fight against war-seasoned veterans of a nation certainly not particularly inclined to the arts of peace.

That they did not succeed altogether, and that the young Prussian soldiers did not always stand up to their enemy as their fathers before them had done at Ligny, is not much wondered at: the marvel is that they succeeded so well. My readers will, I am sure, believe that it is not my intention to underrate the fighting power of the Germans as a race, yet if any good is to be derived from the study of their experiences, it is necessary to tell a good many home truths about the matter. No one who has knocked about the world at all requires to be told that there is more fight about the individual Anglo-Saxon than about any other nationality.

At sea, though the English sailor has the worst reputation for drunkenness and insubordination of any race, yet in times of danger he is, in the opinion of the most trustworthy witnesses, decidedly the most reliable—and this is equally the case wherever you take him on shore. The striking point about him is his individuality, and, unlike any other race in the world, he shows to most advantage when thrown on his own resources, and least when one of a crowd—just the characteristics which should tell most with the breech-loader. It does not take many years or even months in Germany to discover that there the opposite rule holds good; in this respect the Frenchman is generally a better man than the German.

Again, the habits of the Germans, when not under arms (i. e., before joining the ranks and after entering the reserve), are distinctly not of a kind to develop the military virtues. Compare the amusements of the middle and lower classes in two great manufacturing towns in the two countries—the Germans themselves are fain to admit our advantage—and taking a still lower stratum, that of the agricultural classes from which the bulk of the German recruits are drawn, and we have Prince Hohenlohe's own evidence to show how low the standard of intelligence amongst these actually is, in spite of the greater spread of board-school education amongst them. I will quote but two instances he gives, though these must be taken as extreme cases. One man whom he questioned could count up to eleven, and had heard of seventeen and twenty, but had no definite conception of what the words meant; and another, whom he asked whether he could tell him when "*Der Alte Fritz*" died (about the equivalent of our reference to Queen Anne's decease), replied that he thought it might have happened "last week."

Such supreme instances of imbecility have never come my way, but I have seen many hundreds of recruits of both nations, and have never in my life known one of ours quite as dull and wanting in a comprehension of military things as many dozens of Germans. It is not that our average of education is higher, for I have met many of our own recruits who could neither read nor write, whereas it is very seldom one finds such a one in Germany; yet even these all possessed a certain amount of shrewdness and character that was lacking in the others. The individuality of our men is the point I wish to bring forward, and I have made many experiments to prove it, and have found that, even after spending many consecutive days on the range or parade-grounds of German troops, it was still very hard to understand how their officers ever got to know the men apart. Whereas with British, and in a less degree with native troops, there is not the same stamp of uniformity about their features.

With the same object in view, I have collected photographs of groups of men—squads of recruits photographed together—and have submitted then to the inspection of others, who have all noticed the difference. The Germans have, of course, one great advantage over us, in that the liability to universal service, enables them to attain a level average of physique and intellect, whereas we are compelled to put up with a tail; but, judging the men by the mean, and not by the extreme specimens of either, I have long since come to the conclusion that our raw material is better than theirs.

And yet with this initial advantage on our side, and seven years instead of three to train it, the manufactured article we turn out does not compare at all favourably, in point of discipline and smartness under arms, with that of the Germans of today, (as at time of first publication); and if history is in any way a guide, these two characteristics are the indispensable qualifications of good fighting troops.

No doubt it might prove that, in spite of these drawbacks, we would still, thanks to our native fighting instinct, give as good an account of ourselves on the battlefield, but no reasonable man can doubt that without them we should be very much better still; and no soldier should be content to rest till, at any rate, his own command are able to compare with any others in all respects. That it is not so, I take to be due to the fact that our copy of the German system is in the main a very imperfect one. The keystone of the whole structure of organisation with them lies in the subdivision of the work and the delegation of responsibility.

No man of ordinary capacity can command more than a certain number of individuals, the limit of which lies somewhere between 100 and 200, for it is, humanly speaking, impossible to know more than that number sufficiently thoroughly to command well; but within these limits a man may reasonably be expected to know each man under him, as regards temper, character, etc., sufficiently to be able to manage them to the greatest possible advantage; and having been given his command, he must be prepared to stand or fall by his success or failure with it.

These two conditions are fulfilled in the case of the German captain, and in so far he is better off than our own; but after that begin his difficulties, and these lie, much as with us, principally in the selection of the non-commissioned officers. Every single obstacle that we encounter he encounters too, only it is generally several times bigger. In spite of the national pride in their great army, which every German feels after his service in it is over, the individual does not at the time feel his share in the glorious whole sufficiently vividly, and shows but little desire to re-engage in it. Notably is this the case with the men of higher education, who know the market value of their brains. Hence it follows that only those who are not very confident in their own ability to make their careers can be induced to re-engage, and it is hardly necessary to point out that this residuum of a race which is nowhere remarkable for individuality of character does not possess many of the qualifications of the born leaders of men; and, as a rule, they are *afraid of responsibility*.

I was once at a Brighton volunteer review in company with a German officer, an old and intimate friend, who spoke the truth without the slightest regard to my national vanity whenever he felt inclined, but this time his remarks were most flattering. It was at the crises of the fight, firing and confusion were at their greatest height, when suddenly the defenders rose up and made a counter-attack in almost perfect form—as a matter of tactics it was certainly wrong, but in execution it left nothing to be desired. But the enemy met it in the same way—the sections beyond the immediate front wheeled inwards, and fired into their flanks, and presently they had to retire and take up their former position, from which they were eventually driven out, followed by the assailants, who were working instinctively in little sections of four or five men, one of whom gave his orders to his comrades, and was obeyed by them, even though he was in many cases only a private like themselves.

This was what struck my friend most in the whole day's work, and he exclaimed: "Why, each of those men is more intelligent than one of our non-commissioned officers," and I have since had ample reason to agree with him. The fact is, the Englishman is unequalled at, to use a Yankeeism, "bossing a show." You have only to give him a little practice and a certain amount of authority, and he will manage to acquit himself of his task at any rate more satisfactorily than any other man. I have often since, when going round large siege works at night or by day, noticed young sapper recruits of less than two years' service quietly "bossing" their working parties of twenty or thirty men with all the cool self-possession of a commissioned officer, and there is no particularly marked intellectual superiority about the sapper over his comrades of the line.

No, as regards material for non-commissioned officers, the German captain is decidedly at a disadvantage as compared with ours, but he has an advantage in the fact that as he is allowed practically a free choice in the selection of them, his own vital interests lead him to choose the best he can, and neither the regulations nor the customs of the service permit his selections to be ridden over by the orderly room. Such scandals as are still so frequent amongst us, of a teetotal or tub-thumping colonel forcing his own men upon a captain, would be simply inconceivable in Germany; and it follows that a captain takes a far keener interest in his work, knowing he is not likely to be made a fool of in this way, than he can reasonably be expected to do under our system. But even when he has chosen his non-commissioned officers, the German captain's troubles are by no means at an end—he and his subalterns have to teach them their duties, and this in itself is no easy task; and, lastly, the instructors have to be confronted with their men as they come up fresh from the plough, so to speak.

I have already noticed above how very far short of a respectable standard some of these fall, but what is even more striking is their extraordinary clumsiness in the use of their limbs. The English agricultural recruit is not limber in his movements either, but he is an acrobat compared to the German, who literally has to be taught to jump over a ditch 3 feet wide. Prince Hohenlohe again is an authority to consult on this head, and one who cannot be suspected of anti-national bias. But now we come to the difference in the principle of instruction. The primary object the Germans have in view is the training of the *will* of the soldier: he is to be taught to concentrate his thought on the performance of his duty, and that to the utmost possible extent. By easy steps he is first given command of his limbs, and then he is made to execute the movements laid down with the utmost concentrated energy of his will.

This was formerly the idea in our own service, and is still in our navy, but the tacticians have changed all that; and besides, thanks to our organisation, we lack the one commanding will at the head of each company, for our captains have not the overmastering incentive to exertion that the German ones have. Every German company commander is compelled to infuse his whole soul into his subordinates, for he knows his whole subsequent career depends entirely on his doing so, and with the same incentive to exertion the British captain would do so too. Besides this, by tradition, a faith has grown up in the army in the efficacy of this smartness under arms, that nothing now can shake; they know that no forms of tactical employment or perfection of arms are of any avail, unless they have some power behind them to enable the men to overcome their natural disinclination for extreme danger, and that power they find to consist in the concentrated wills of all under their command, who from the very first are taught how to concentrate their wills on the execution of the given order

With us this idea appears to have almost died out, and instruction has taken its place; men are to be taught many things, but to insist on the execution of any of them with this complete concentration of effort is thought to be needlessly harassing to the men, and therefore to be discouraged as leading to desertion. And, finally, there is the fundamental distinction between the two systems which has crept in since the last war—namely, that the Germans believe that the first object of military instruction is to teach the soldier to know *how to die*, and we teach him *how to avoid dying*. What the result of the latter system was in Germany before 1870, the *Midsummer-Night's Dream* will show; but though the Germans have not gone so far as the writer of that particular pamphlet would have them do, yet they are at present far ahead of us in that respect, and far ahead of what they were in 1870. From 1866 to about 1876 the main idea of extended order in the army was the avoidance of loss.

Since 1876 about, it has become the infliction of loss on the enemy; and though the men are still trained to skirmish individually, yet, as the writer of the above mentioned pamphlet pointed out, their individual freedom to avail themselves of cover in the attack has been curtailed to such an extent that to all intents and purposes they might as well be in close-order line (single rank) again. The main point with them now is to impress on the troops that the only way to avoid loss oneself is to inflict heavier loss on the enemy, and every consideration of personal safety must give way to this necessity.

28

Surely these ideas are far better suited to our national proclivities than the opposite ones, and if on these lines it is possible to turn out good troops from such unpromising materials as we have seen the Germans have to work up inside of three years, cannot we, by adopting them, do something better in seven years than we are now doing? Smartness, which results from the direct example of the officers themselves, and which is maintained by pride and feeling of esprit de corps and not by punishment, makes men contented and disinclined to desert; but I maintain that such smartness can only be attained by dividing up the men into such fractions that the officers may know them all personally, and that the officer must stand or fall by the use he makes of that knowledge.

I firmly believe that the moment it became known that promotion to the rank of field officer depended primarily on the smartness and efficiency of his company or troop under arms, as judged by an independent board, and not on his proficiency in book-learning, we should see an astounding improvement in the fruit of our short service, and in a few years' time might laugh at the Germans. But the officers must be allowed to control their companies for a little longer than six weeks in a year.

The Napoleonic Conscription

A valuable pamphlet has been Issued by the *Militaer Wochenblatt* in which the conditions under which Napoleon raised his armies, and the sort of men he had to deal with, are made the subject of an extremely searching historical investigation, and this investigation supplies us with a mass of information of the greatest importance to those who are trying to trace the gradual process of development of modern tactics. Everyone who has given even a little thought to this most important subject must have been puzzled to account for the extraordinary phenomenon that whereas theorists, even the soundest, have almost from the introduction of firearms preached the superiority of individual order over close order as a form of infantry combat, and that though the theorists have been admitted to have had right on their side, by many, if not by all, of the greatest leaders, yet these same leaders have in practice again and again been compelled to have recourse to the latter method; and the ordinary common-sense practical soldiers, particularly the regimental officers, have always been at open war with the pamphleteers.

The explanation of the matter appears to be, that experience has proved that tactical forms should be based on the nature of the man, and not on the weapon he carries: and that the great leaders, being executive officers, have had to content themselves, not with the theoretically best form, but with what their experience taught them could be practically accomplished by the men they had to deal with; and in this they have been supported by the bulk of the regimental officers, who, being in immediate contact with the men, knew what the latter were capable of accomplishing, and never troubled their heads with schemes, often far beyond the comprehension of many of them, based on what might be done with ideally perfect material: in short, the "tacticians were not soldiers enough, and the soldiers not tacticians enough"—a saying which precisely hits the point of the warfare between the two sects which has been raging in the British Army for the last twenty years.

The history of the Napoleonic infantry and cavalry tactics is a precise record, which shows the gradual deterioration of the fighting value of the recruits supplied; and had the last Franco-German War continued as an obstinately fought out struggle for several years, I believe that the German method of employing their forces would have followed the same steps in principle, though in detail, distances, etc., they would of course have largely varied. This actually did take place during the American Civil War to a considerable extent, and with longer time would have gone further; and there are not wanting indications that this idea has largely influenced the course of German tactics during the last fifteen years.

The history of this idea is briefly this: wherever long-service armies existed, and especially in such countries as were too poor or too miserly to pay their men well, service in the army was decidedly unpopular. In countries in which the burden of military service fell exclusively on the poorest classes, the army lost caste with the nation, and, being shamefully treated by the civilian element, gradually became divorced from the country, and if called out to fight, was usually utterly devoid of patriotism, and not in the least anxious to fight to the last drop of their blood in defence of the institutions of its fatherland, for which for the most part they felt the most profound indifference.

The tendency to desert on the march and in camp, and to skulk in action, was accordingly very great indeed, and it became therefore impossible to trust these men before the enemy, except under the immediate eye of their officers; and this reason alone compelled Frederick the Great to adhere to his line tactics, which were copied by us slavishly, though, as the history of the light division sufficiently proves, the same causes did not exist, to anything like the same extent But, though not to the same extent, they certainly did exist, do exist, and will continue to exist as long as our army—or rather, the individual members of it who wear the Queen's uniform—are treated with the same disdain by the civilians, and till we can succeed in attracting a higher average class of men to the colours; and amateur army-reformers would do well to bear this point in mind.

Against troops recruited and maintained in the same manner, and not so well drilled, the line tactics succeeded gloriously, both in our own and the Prussian service; but where pitted against nations who rose spontaneously in arms and fought for freedom, or what they thought would give them freedom, they failed completely, both in our own case in America and in the Prussian case against Revolutionary France. The tactics employed by both countries were the same—not having drill or training enough to meet the line in open field, they attacked it as far as possible in broken ground and in skirmishes. And against the Prussians in France in 1792 a form of fighting was evolved by experiment identical with that the Germans subsequently employed in 1870—namely, dense swarms of skirmishers backed by small columns. But the essential feature on which the possibility of this style of fighting hinged was the presence in the ranks of a sufficient number of individually brave men who went into the skirmishing or fighting line and stayed there, either because they liked it, or from higher motives: and men of this stamp were numerous at the outbreak of the Revolutionary wars.

The Revolutionary fever, however, soon spent itself, and already before Napoleon became First Consul the Committee of National Defence was very hard put to it to find men for their armies. In 1789 General Jourdan brought before the Council of Five Hundred the first draft of a conscription bill, which, though it eventually became law, was most bitterly opposed as contrary to the principles of the Republic. At first the conscription was universal and for five years' service, though it soon became practically for life; and as a means of raising money the principle of paid substitutes was sanctioned. It was not popular from the beginning, and a very large percentage of decidedly unwilling conscripts were in the ranks of the Grand Army that fought at Austerlitz and Jena, but the strong leaven of old Republicans, and the force of tradition and drill, still rendered it possible to apply the skirmishing tactics successfully on both those battlefields.

But the Spanish and Calabrian insurrections, and the terrible hardships and frightful cruelties the insurgents perpetrated on the French who fell into their hands, soon rendered it a tax beyond the patience of the nation to endure, and if the nation was quick to resent it, it may be imagined what the unlucky States incorporated into the confederation of the Rhine, and the Italians, thought of it. In Spain whole regiments melted away; the Westphalian contingent which crossed the Pyrenees in 1809 were reduced to a single battalion by April, 1810. A Saxon regiment that left Mannheim on the 18th of January, 1810, with 32 officers and 1,194 men, and which was further reinforced in April by 38 officers and 1,229 men, mustered in November of the same year

Charge of the Mamelukes at Austerlitz

only 16 officers and 7 men fit for duty, and of the whole number who crossed the Rhine only 38 officers and 249 men succeeded in reaching Germany again. The little duchy of Berg lost 12,000 of its male inhabitants in Spain alone.

As regards cruelties, both Calabrians and Spaniards had nothing to learn from the Afghans, or even from the Inquisition, but mutilated the wounded and tortured the prisoners with all possible refinements of cruelty. The impression created by these lessons and losses spread with the proverbial rapidity for which bad news is notorious, and the resistance against the conscription, which had been steadily growing, became rapidly desperate. Where in 1806 the percentage of absentees had been about 25, it rose in 1809-10 to upwards of 80, and it was precisely in these departments which had previously provided the best men for individual fighting (as opposed to mass fighting) that the result was most serious, for it required considerable self-reliance of character in the individual to dare the authorities and expose himself to all the consequences of being an outlaw.[1]

A further result, of course, was that the men who stayed were for the most part the least likely to make good soldiers. The men sent up to the front to reinforce the army of Austria before Wagram were of such an unreliable nature that it was considered necessary in the battle of Wagram to form the whole infantry of MacDonald's corps in one huge column, each line of which consisted of deployed battalions, closed to six paces' distance, and some fourteen battalions deep. This monstrous formation was only repeated on one subsequent occasion, and then through a misunderstood order at Waterloo, where the column thus formed was charged and ridden over by the Union Brigade, who brought in some 5,000 prisoners.

Another essential factor which led to the use of these heavy columns—a point which deserves to be specially borne in mind by would-be reformers—was the fact that from Jena onwards the confidence of the French infantry in themselves had been dangerously shaken by the stubbornness of the resistance they had encountered in the open field. They had encountered foemen, man for man, fully their equals, and only the masterly employment of the artillery under Senarmont had given them the very incomplete victories of Eylau and Friedland, and naturally it was felt that what the old veteran troops had failed to perform was beyond the power of the riff-raff now being supplied to them.

---

1. *Vide* Buchanan's *Shadow of the Sword.*

BATTLE OF EYLAU

The result of the employment of these heavy columns only made matters worse, for the losses increased in enormous proportions, and the drain on the country was still further augmented. In order to try and beat up the "*refractaires*," as they were called, no less than sixteen flying columns, numbering some 82,000 infantry and cavalry, were employed in France alone, and the men of these columns were quartered on the inhabitants of the villages from which men liable to service had escaped, and authorised to behave as if they were in the enemy's country.

The men they brought in were placed in irons, and when a sufficient number had been got together, they were marched out into the country for a few miles, formed in three sides of a square, and a percentage of men selected by lot were shot before their eyes, "*pour encourager les autres.*" The remainder were then marched down to the coast in chain gangs, and taken by ship to the islands of Oléron, Rhé, and Walcheren, and others suitably situated, where they were organised in battalions by specially selected officers, who were ordered literally to coax them into a good humour again, for Napoleon thoroughly understood that the more obstinate the "*refractaire*" the more likely he was to make a good soldier eventually, if once he could be made fairly contented with his lot.

From the islands they were again taken by ship, when the English cruisers permitted, to ports in Holland, and marched overland, without touching French soil, to their destinations. Of course it was principally the exceptionally determined recalcitrants who were thus dealt with, for all the islands round the French coast would not have been sufficient to afford accommodation for all the deserters. The less obstinate ones were placed in the ordinary *dépôts*, and their spirits broken to discipline by constant drill and hard marching, under which the weaker ones broke down, and only the hardier ones remained to march against the enemy. So that, in spite of all drawbacks, the men who eventually reached the front were in all respects, except as regards training to stand fire, disciplined troops, and not mere recruits.

But whilst in France everything was thus tending to reduce the value of the French infantry and cavalry, things in Germany were going just the opposite way. Under the terrible hardships and oppression the French inflicted on the occupied provinces, a feeling of ardent patriotism was growing up amongst the very men who before the disaster of Jena had been sunk in the very lowest depths of slavish indifference to duty. The civil population of Prussia previous to that event was so thoroughly divorced from the army, and so utterly blind to their own interests, that they went so far as to welcome the invaders, and to cover the remnants of the army, which in spite of incompetent chiefs had so loyally done its best to protect them from invasion, with opprobrium and scorn.

I doubt whether even the modern British Radical news-sheet could sink to such filthy vituperation as the Berlin newspapers of the day indulged in, when first the French marched into the capital; but this state of mind did not last long, for flesh and blood could not stand the French as guests, and, before many months were over, many of the most virulent of them fled to unoccupied portions of the territory and became most whole-souled defenders of their fatherland with their pens, if not with their swords. All over Germany secret societies were formed, the one object of which was to inspire in every member's heart the same fanaticism of despair which animates the Ghazi. When, after the retreat from Russia, the opportunity at length came, these men flocked to the colours by thousands, and, being almost entirely without discipline and drill, adopted almost instinctively the same method of fighting—namely, individual order—as had previously given their victors their superiority.

Of course, too, they were aided in this by the survivors of the old army, who, having seen the result of their previous error, had now rushed into the other extreme, much as our own reformers did after 1870, and now would be satisfied with nothing but skirmishing and loose order; and it was only owing to the exertions of the very men who before 1806 had been foremost in recommending moderate reform, chief amongst whom was Scharnhorst, that enough steady drill was maintained to save the army from degenerating into a horde of savages, which would have been shattered to pieces in the first engagement by the masterly combination of the three arms that Napoleon had now learnt to employ. In this art of combination Napoleon had now reached his zenith, and never in military history have the three arms played into each other's hands so perfectly, each covering the weak point of the other. His battles began by a preliminary deployment of skirmishers all along the front, and, in the gradual development of the struggle, the opposing infantry were led to a premature consumption and movement of their reserves, and a deployment of their artillery.

Then when the enemy had sufficiently shown his hand, an overpowering force of artillery was brought up to case-shot range, which poured in fire considerably heavier than any repeaters of today, (as at time of first publication), could develop, before which no columns or lines could stand; and when their work of preparation was sufficiently completed, a mass of cavalry (such as it was) was, to use an expression of Prince Hohenlohe's, induced to run away in the direction of the enemy, and behind them the massive columns of the infantry marched up to occupy the conquered position, and frequently reached and held it without firing a single shot.

Things, of course, did not always work as smoothly as intended; the enemy flung their cavalry against that of the French, and a more or less unsatisfactory cavalry duel ensued. When this was the case, the following infantry were not always equal to their task, but if they failed, there was left in his hand his final reserve—the Guard; and the strength of these lay almost entirely in their extraordinary capacity for enduring heavy loss. It was indeed fortunate for Prussia that she had still some men left her who retained their heads in the midst of the general confusion of ideas, and had insisted on the necessity of maintaining the highest possible standard of discipline. Without this backbone, the skirmishing hordes would have been totally incapable of opposing the French when handled by Napoleon in person.

It will be seen, therefore, that the tactics of the two opposing forces had changed about. At the outset the French relied almost exclusively on a form of individual fighting of infantry which resulted, by a process of natural selection, from the conditions out of which the Revolutionary armies sprang, and in this order were pretty generally victorious over the rigidly handled Prussians, who, it was said, and with partial truth, by their opponents, were so wanting in all the attributes of free men that they only marched against the enemy because they were more afraid of their officers than of the enemy's bullets. And at the end of the war it was the Prussians and Germans generally who had in turn and in a similar manner developed an "individual order" system, whilst the French infantry had sunk so low that they had almost ceased to fight at all, the whole of their duty being to march up with sloped arms into the positions from which the artillery and cavalry had already driven the enemy.

Now let us apply this reasoning to what happened in the 1870 campaign. The German short-service soldiers, full of confidence in their weapon, and knowing that the best way to utilize it was to get into close quarters (*i. e.,* say within 500 yards), went into the fight with considerable dash and go. But a very few minutes knocked the fight out of a large number of them, who had not been trained to "know how to die, and not how to avoid dying." The ground was covered with skulkers, and, to save the fighting line, the next body of troops was sent into the struggle by the higher leaders. These fared no better; appalled by the sight of the losses around them, and those that were suffering, they too lost their order—the bravest rushed to the front, and the remainder stayed behind.

A third reinforcement, perhaps a fourth and a fifth, followed, till at last, by a process of survival of the fittest, a line of the best men got up to close quarters with the enemy, and by better shooting drove him out of the field. Some corps fought better than others, and in these, particularly the 3rd (Brandenburgers), the straggling was less; but, on the whole, this overhaste was the characteristic of the battles up to the 18th of August (Gravelotte, St. Privat). By this time every corps had been under fire, and had had an opportunity of judging what a needless expenditure of men this style of fighting entailed. They were much soberer at Sédan and waited for the proper deployment of artillery and for the infantry to get into hand previous to attacking. The result was a victory won with a most astonishingly small loss, of about 10 *per cent.*

Though this result was partly due to the diminished fighting-power of their enemy, still, more deliberate leading had much to say to it. This finished the war between organised troops of equal quality, but it is interesting to try and reason out what form the fighting would have taken had the contest been prolonged and a species of equilibrium restored between the contending forces. It is very certain that the Germans were much impressed by the heaviness of the losses they suffered, and that extraordinarily exaggerated reports about them were circulated in the country behind. A series of even slight checks in their career of victory might, and probably would, have speedily damped the ardour of new recruits called up to fill the ranks, and inevitably a time would have arrived when the individual dash of the men could no longer have been counted on to carry them forward, and the same method in principle as that relied on by Napoleon would have had to be reverted to.

Losses or no losses, men would have had to be driven into the fight, and the only hope at length of victory would have lain in the employment of artillery and cavalry on such a scale that again, as in the old days, the infantry might have walked into previously conquered positions with sloped arms. To the German General Staff this ultimate idea has always presented itself, as anyone can satisfy himself by noting carefully the line their tactical development has consistently followed. They have never allowed themselves to be misled by the humanitarian outcry against the appalling losses which formed the bases of the arguments of the pamphleteers, for all along they have been aware that these appalling losses never occurred, and they are also familiar with every line of the original controversy on the subject of close versus individual order which raged at the beginning of the century, but of which our tactical guides appear never to have read a line.

They grant, as everyone will be ready to do, that, given sufficiently brave men, individual order in the fighting line is ideal, and more particularly so since the introduction of the breech-loader; but they have not adopted it as a means to reducing loss in battle, except in so far as it enables the troops employing it to inflict greater loss on the enemy. Precisely the opposite point of view to that taken up by the British school.

They are prepared to derive all the advantage from this form that they can, and their system of individual instruction has for its primary object to develop in the soldier the qualities which will enable him to preserve the requisite courage and self-reliance, without which it is impossible. But they have never lost sight of the prospect that they may have to fight battles with men who do not possess these qualifications, and then, though even in their own army there is a tremendous schism against them in the junior ranks, the leaders (those who have seen war) axe determined, if the necessity arises, and if the men decline to win in individual order with a loss of only say 20 *per cent* on an average; to drive them into action and force them to win in close order, even if it cost 50 *per cent,* the price Napoleon paid for Wagram; of course, like him, seeking to diminish the calls on the infantry by the unsparing use of artillery and cavalry.

No matter what perfection the armament attains to, its ultimate power on the battlefield depends on the nerves and courage of the men to whom it is entrusted. Artillery has, relatively speaking, no nerves, for the gun and the ground never shake, and besides, the detachments are, so to speak, anchored to the ground. The greater the torrent of projectiles poured out, the greater becomes the necessity for speed in the advance, and that speed will always be found in the cavalry, which arm also has the advantage, thanks to its superior mobility, of being kept out of fire till wanted, and then appearing, with its morale not only unshaken, but positively intensified by the rapid motion of the charge.

No matter what pitch of perfection firearms attain, these two fundamental advantages will remain on the side of the cavalry and artillery, and though we never expect to see again on any European battlefields soldiers so entirely demoralized *ab initio* as were the latter-day soldiers of the Empire, still the more the volume of modern fire is increased, and the greater the distances it sweeps, the more certain does it become that eventually such a state of moral collapse will set in, and the only way to guard against its effects on one's own side, or to draw advantage from them on that of the enemy, will be by assigning larger duties to the cavalry and artillery, and making the most of the above mentioned two fundamental advantages they possess.

I do not wish to be understood to be desirous of exalting any one arm at the expense of the other, but I claim an equal right for all. An army forms a trinity in which none is before or after the other, none is greater or less than the other; and the country whose leaders are the first to recognize this great truth will be as invincible on land as Napoleon was, till he met a leader backed by better men who understood this fundamental truth even better than he did himself.

The Old Peninsular Army

It is well known throughout the service, thanks principally to the necessity of study on the part of officers anxious for promotion, or the Staff College, that the British infantry who fought in the Peninsula earned from the best and ablest of their opponents, *e. g.*, Napoleon, Bugeaud, and Foy—the high praise of being the best in the world; but to form a true estimate of what the ultimate fighting value of British troops might be, it is well to remember out of what elements it was composed, and under what disadvantages of organisation and tradition it fought. As regards material, it is pretty generally known that the standard of height, physique, and still more of character, fell very far short of what we require today; but we live so fast nowadays, and are so busy in slaying the unfortunate Prussian Guards over again in order to form a foundation for new systems of attack formations, that we are in danger of forgetting the other factors of the case.

In a very old copy of *Fraser's Magazine*, dated September, 1833, I have found an admirable article from the pen of the late General Mitchell (R. A.), which gives a singularly good idea of what the old army was, and which I think will probably interest my readers, for I take it that such information is invaluable to all who wish to form an independent view as to the capabilities of British troops. As regards the formation or reconstruction of the military machine, he says:

> When in 1803, after a disastrous waste of blood and treasure, it became apparent, even to the meanest capacity, that an efficient engine of war was absolutely necessary, every exertion was made to metamorphose Englishmen into soldiers—a task that the Whigs assured us was altogether hopeless. As pipeclay and drill were in those days looked upon as the best specifics for teaching Britons—the boldest and most athletic men in Europe— how to fight, an officer had then a fair chance of be-

ing promoted provided he could strut up and down a parade in a commanding manner, give his orders in a loud voice, and, above all, make a battalion perform, in a cloud of pipeclay and hair-powder dust, some of the so-called 'eighteen manoeuvres.' A good deal of abuse heaped upon all ranks of subordinates was passed over, and became almost fashionable, whilst the foolish pedantry with which a number of high officials watched over the details of dress made an officer almost dependent on his tailor and hatter for the tenure of his commission.

As to military talents, they were by universal consent never spoken of; they were deemed far beyond our grasp, and accessible only to our enemies; all military knowledge open to Englishmen was supposed to be confined to the book of regulations. If anyone ever thought about the higher branches of the science, he carefully kept such thoughts to himself, well knowing that, right or wrong, they would at best have been considered as *de tres mauvais ton*; and as to writing on the subject, it was, of course, utterly out of the question. Nor is there a single work or essay on military affairs dating from the commencement of the war that is even worth the paper on which it is printed. The Horse Guards, so favourably distinguished for courtesy in all official transactions, almost forgot their usual politeness if anybody attempted to bring matters' of professional science to their notice.

It is a curious fact that none of the officers of the martinet school distinguished themselves in the field, or acquired any permanent reputation, whilst many were eminently unfortunate. The late Sir Henry Clinton was nearly the only exception: he was a man of the highest military talent, perfectly acquainted indeed with all the details of duty, but likely to be strict only about those which were of real importance. As a general he commanded the divisions which decided both at Salamanca and Waterloo.

No one was more free from the martinet mania than the Duke himself; he hardly ever interfered with the drill and exercise of the troops, and in matters of dress gave the officers pretty nearly *carte blanche*. The martinet dynasty was also favourable to the rise of what were termed in the army 'pen and ink' men— not, as might be supposed, literary characters, but staff officers, mostly brigade majors and *aides-de-camp*, who could make out a neat return, quote page and chapter of a regulation, and who knew the number of a manoeuvre without perhaps knowing its object, could write a neat invitation to dinner, and a vapid brigade order after an inspection. Of these only one cut a figure during the war.

About the same time a good many foreign adventurers—counts and barons, of course—obtained rank amongst us. under pretence of being heirs to the high military wisdom and science deemed by universal accord, completely beyond the reach of Englishmen. They brought us 'filthy' moustaches, fur caps, and fantastic hussar jackets; and, having drawn good pay and pensions, passed away without leaving a single name sufficiently remembered to be laughed at. None of these adventurers belonged to the King's German Legion. The officers of that corps were mostly Hanoverians, men of rank in their own country and generally also of good education; and, taken as a body, could not be surpassed by any corps of officers whatever.

It is well known that, owing to the exertions of the Whigs and other Opposition parties of the day, the British Army took the field at the commencement of the Peninsula War totally destitute of all confidence except what was derived from the undisputed courage of the individuals of whom it was composed. It was weighed down by the belief in some mighty phantom of military science that, at the command of our enemies, was to descend upon us in thunder and crush our puny efforts. To this phantom, that was always coming but never came, we thought we could oppose nothing but hard, stubborn fighting, and, the infantry under this narrow view having been brought once front to front with the enemy, the result was pretty generally trusted to the gallantry of the troops: and their gallantry was never trusted in vain.

We do not know that the British troops ever fought with any advantage on their side beyond what they derived from their own sterling qualities, but they frequently fought at a great disadvantage, and not a single battle from 1808 to 1814 can be mentioned in which, had the parties changed sides, the results would not have been exactly reversed. 1,500 French would not; have driven 8,000 British from the field of Albuera, and the attempt to escalade Badajos and storm Ciudad Rodrigo would have been laughed to scorn. From this it follows that our success was due far more to the gallantry, good conduct, and high feeling pervading alike all ranks of the army, than to the skill and exertion of any particular class.

Then follows a long dissertation on the way in which the services of the regimental officers and the men were rewarded, very interesting, but too long for quotation; the concluding remarks are, however, necessary to understand what our author goes on to say about the way the men fought.

The minds of all officers were literally fettered, no one was supposed even capable of thinking on military matters: there was no professional assimilation of feeling; no amalgamation of sentiment, beyond what honour, patriotism, or private friendship inspired, ever took place. We were kept together by the iron bonds of a stern and rigid discipline, tempered only by the zeal and goodwill that avowedly pervaded all ranks. The injurious consequences of this estrangement extended themselves like a damp, chilling mist over the whole profession; affecting more particularly the cavalry, who are more dependent on the daring and spirit of enterprise of individuals.

The men followed their generals mechanically; some leaders were better liked than others, some cordially hated, but none exercised any commanding influence over the minds of either officers or privates. Colonel Napier, in describing the critical situation of the army after the Battle of Albuera, says that the men had lost all confidence in their leaders. There was plenty of despondency and want of confidence (as to results) in the army on the evening of the battle of Waterloo; but it never shook the resolution of the men. On the contrary, it brought on that stubborn and resolved kind of fierceness that, after any desperate and protracted resistance, seizes on the minds of British soldiers, and makes them callous to all but *the desire of destroying their enemies.*

On ordinary occasions, when soldiers assist their wounded officers or comrades to the rear, they return—when they do return at all—leisurely enough; but at Waterloo many of them refused to quit the ranks, and others actually left wounded officers in the middle of the road, and then returned to their posts. But all this was totally independent of any opinion entertained of their commanders. They were fierce and anxious to

avenge their comrades.

Whoever had opportunities of seeing British troops engaged, or ever beheld such men as the Duke of Wellington, the Marquis of Anglesey, Lords Hill, Hopetoun, Lynedoch, Sir Hussey Vivian, and a host of others under fire, could not fail to be struck with the abundance of that high spirit in the army which counts life and toil as nothing when weighed against the honour and interest of the country. *Nearly* all those who at any time held responsible command in action looked as if it would have been impossible to make them comprehend the existence of anything like personal danger to themselves; the minds even of the least composed and tranquil (and some were, owing to an intense anxiety about results, far from tranquil) appeared incapable of descending to such considerations.

Then follows a very long nominal list of regimental officers, and he then proceeds to back up his favourite theory of the advantage of a good military education, and—probably also with a certain amount of personal bias, being himself a gunner—to speak of the artillery in the following terms:

In this army list *raisonne* we must pass over the artillery, for few officers of that arm could be altogether named without praise— which shows how much a good military education, such as they had all enjoyed, is sure to effect. The artillery formed, in fact, the most perfect branch of the Peninsular Army, and was, of course, free from the shackles that modern tactics had so successfully imposed on both cavalry and infantry. The engineers were unpopular—undeservedly so, we think, for a corps that reckoned such men as Jones, Fletcher, and Paisley in its ranks could not easily be surpassed.

Next to the artillery, and far superior to the rest of the infantry, by their morale alone, were the Light Division. They had been trained under Sir John Moore to a better and more efficient system of tactics than any other part of the line; and as they were generally in advance and nearest the enemy, they contrived to rid themselves more effectually than the rest of the army of the trammels that the modern science of war has so carefully imposed upon military talent and energy. This sort of freedom, backed by success, produced in all ranks a degree of pride and confidence that led to the best results, and proved on every occasion how vastly superior *British soldiers are in point of professional intelligence to the best of Continental troops*. (The italics are my own.)

Nothing indeed could exceed the aptitude of the men in this division, in whatever related to actual duty, except the buoyant extravagance of spirits they displayed whenever they were released from restraint. In their sayings and doings they approached nearer to the manner of sailors than any other troops in the army, and proved beyond dispute that to an Englishman war is by far the most congenial pursuit. It is only '*on rolling oceans or in fighting fields*' that the spirits of our countrymen are really awakened; the ordinary occupations of life seem unable to call forth all the energy of their nature. With such men trained on a system doing justice to their qualities, the conquest of the world were yet an easy task.

As regards the cavalry—and on this subject General Mitchell deserves to be heard, for he has written most ably on cavalry tactics, and thoroughly understands his subject—he says:

It was allowed on all hands that their contribution to the general success bore a small proportion to the quantum of reward bestowed on them. In Sir John Moore's campaign, indeed, they carried everything before them; and had they always acted up to the standard then established, it is difficult to say what would have equalled their deserts; but their ill-success at Talavera, which must not, however, be altogether placed to their account, completely damped their ardour.

The spirit of victory that flashed along the line the moment the order was given at Salamaca for the whole to advance, communicated itself to the cavalry, and they made one gallant and effective charge during the battle, and another during the pursuit; but they again fell off during the retreat from Burgos, and Vittoria was their darkest day, for they allowed the broken French infantry to get away when they ought to have destroyed them. It is not easy to generalise the conduct of the cavalry at Waterloo. Ponsonby's brigade made a noble, we may say a tremendous, charge, for it swept at least ten thousand men from the ground, and Vivian's brigade gave the *coup de grace*, though the battle was then, perhaps, no longer doubtful.

There is a great deal more of interesting matter which might be quoted if space permitted, but I think I have extracted enough to give anyone an idea of what the old army was like which won us our reputation; and I think the reflection must occur to all, that if under such disadvantageous circumstances we could do so well, what might we not have achieved with higher organisation, a more capable staff, and an army uncontaminated with the jail-birds and other undesirable characters who too freely found their way into its ranks.

Our army today, (as at time of first publication), though far from being the pick of the nation as it should be, is at least free from the first of these reproaches, is better organised, and the staff are fairly educated; and at any rate, no matter what party may be in power, it is never likely to be treated as disgracefully as its forerunner was in the matter of supplies and equipment. But it is wanting in one thing, which the old army had in the highest degree, and that is *the knowledge how to die*. Instead of that, we have been sedulously taught for the last twenty years the *art of knowing how to avoid dying*, and it can hardly be maintained that twenty years of this *régime* is calculated to stiffen the backbone of any troops.

A similar system was far from having a favourable effect on the German troops in the interval between 1866 and 1870, though with them the sound common sense of the leaders prevented the dogma attaining such colossal dimensions as it has done in our own service; and since the war, at any rate for the last fifteen years, the positive object—namely, to adopt extended order as a means of killing the enemy, and not as a means of avoiding loss oneself—has been the basis of their instruction. General Mitchell's testimony to the qualifications of the Light Division is to my mind the strongest proof that as a nation we possess the requisite individuality for fighting in extended order to a greater degree than any other race, and we may, perhaps, safely go farther in this direction than others, but only by following the Germans again and insisting on the positive object—namely, the infliction of loss, not its avoidance.

But modern firearms have in so far altered the conditions since the Peninsula times that we are nowadays compelled to march men across a fire-swept zone of, say, 2,000 paces' depth, and, while doing so, the troops are unable to defend themselves by their own fire, because of the fighting line in front; and therefore we require to lay greater stress than ever on the most rigid discipline in these troops, and experience has shown most abundantly the value of the line formation, as a means to the end.

To talk, lecture, and demonstrate the avoidance of loss to the men is certainly not the way to inculcate passive endurance, but since in any general action where the troops are present on the ground at the rate of ten to twelve men to the pace, and since it is evident that only one man at a time can use his rifle with effect on that amount of front, some nine-tenths of all the men put in have to endure loss without replying to it for a considerable portion of the time; the chance any particular body of infantry has of finding itself in a position to skirmish for the whole of an action is very much less than that which it has of having to stand up quietly to be shot at, and under these circumstances it would be wise to dwell a little more on the means of enabling them to do so than has of late years been our practice.

I think all soldiers will agree with me that if the men were not told beforehand that the breech-loader or repeater, as the case may be, is an extremely dangerous weapon, the only point on which they would lay any stress would be the amount of death-dealing fragments or projectiles they would have to face in a given distance or time, for their common sense would tell them that to the man lying on the ground with a bullet through his lungs it is matter of profound indifference whether the bullet came initially from a "ten-*rupee jezail*" or from the latest patent Männlicher repeater—unless, indeed, the man was sufficiently well informed as to know the relative killing powers of the two weapons; and if so, he would know that his chance of recovery in the latter case was a good deal better than it would have been in the former.

And therefore, if British troops have faced, and faced victoriously, a greater storm of projectiles from old smooth-bore guns firing grape, and old muskets sending out 12- or 14-bore leaden bullets, they can equally well face anything that under modern tactical conditions they are likely to be confronted with—always provided their moral courage has not been previously tampered with. They have faced such fire again and again; for instance, at Badajos the fire of 14 heavy smooth-bore pieces, 18- and 24-pounders, raking them on either flank, did not stop them, though the obstacles in front did. In the Crimea, in the assault of the Redan, the converging fire of close on a hundred heavy guns, firing case, also failed to stop them; and at Chillianwalla, Sobraon, and later again at Lucknow, they had to face a storm of bullets and grape-shot far in excess of what modern repeaters at equal odds can ever bring to bear against them, and on all these occasions they were formed shoulder to shoulder in the good old line.

All these instances prove to me conclusively that British troops, trained to know how to die, and not how to avoid dying, are capable of answering to any demands that may be made of them. Let us give our men the best weapons that money can procure by all means, only do not let us teach them that death in itself is any the more terrible because it is delivered by a .298 patent repeating nickel-coated bullet driven by smokeless and noiseless hypernitrated powder.

A nation whose troops less than a century ago proved themselves capable of winning against losses of over 50 *per cent* in individual cases, is capable of turning out equally good ones today, for the fighting instinct is the slowest of all to alter—always provided they are adequately trained; and if they are so trained, then nothing on the continent of Europe can defeat them—still less in Asia.

The Home Army

Army organisation is not the growth of a night. It has taken a century almost for the German nation to work out the complete consequences of a change from long to short service, and her conditions are simple as compared with ours. Judged by that standard, I consider our progress fairly satisfactory. In 1870, had we been called on to go to war, we should practically have had no reserve whatever. Now we have not only 60,000 men of the regular reserve to fall back on, but behind that are some 400,000 trained soldiers, still of an age to bear arms efficiently, and of whom almost the whole might on an emergency be rendered available. This alone is a considerable gain. It would, however, have been far larger by this time had we not had to work against a resistance due partly to the really admirable sentiment that pervaded the officers as a body, which sentiment became hurtful when transplanted to new and strange conditions.

This may seem a contradiction, but it is not so. Had our officers possessed less pride in the splendid old battalions they belonged to or commanded, had they looked on the service merely as a convenient arrangement for supplying bread and butter to themselves, the reforms introduced would have met with little opposition. So long as their pay was secure, they would have contented themselves with drawing it as it became due, and performing their duties in a more or less perfunctory manner. Some of them did so. Being, however, Englishmen, they for the most part took the matter differently.

Their pride was touched, and since their individual training under the old long-service traditions practically precluded them from any thorough grasp of the subject, they took the last of the old regiments they had seen as the normal, ignoring all others which in war time had not come up to the ideal—and many had not done so— and insisted on looking on the new battalions of recruits as the war equivalent to the old ones, which they never could have been, nor were intended to be.

Then, too, as the haze of time passed over all, they began to improve on figures, and if one were to believe all one heard, the old battalions were, every man of them, veritable sons of Anak, no man under 5 feet 11 inches, or less than 40 inches round the chest. As a fact, they never were anything of the kind at starting, though after their ranks had been thinned by a death-rate of 60 per 1,000 against the present 12 per 1,000 in India, the survivors were undoubtedly very fine specimens. They ignored altogether the miserable weeds that had to be enlisted to keep these regiments up to strength whenever the strain of war came upon them. The original returns, however, are still there to remind them, and from these it appears that the old E. I. C. regiments were glad enough during the last year of the Mutiny to take younger and smaller men than ever reach the country nowadays, and to pay them a high bounty for coming.

The special evil of the long-service system, was, and always will be, the impossibility it entails of securing a thorough practical training and knowledge amongst the officers themselves. A man can teach only what he knows; but when there is no necessity to learn, and the men know very much more by practical experience than the young officer, there is not only no incentive to work, but the keenest find least to work at. Given a generation of peace, and it is a moral certainty that not only will the men know nothing of war, but the officers will know even less, for the tradition of the guard-room is a more living force than the tradition of the mess, of which fact I have had ample proof.

Had we, as an army, seen the fighting of 1870, our national common sense would have asserted itself, and we should have realised that there was nothing very novel about it. But we did not see it, and the army being exceedingly modest, as becomes brave men, and conscious of its ignorance, swallowed wholesale the nostrums provided by a limited number of specialists, who, with three or four exceptions, were ambitious men, but wanting in the one essential factor of good officers—namely, the power really to command men. One of them could never be trusted to march his battery to church and back without getting them into a tangle; another I have seen myself tie his command up inextricably under the Duke's own eyes, though he was almost a European authority on matters of strategy; yet another never even commanded a section by word of mouth in his whole service, and a dozen other instances might easily be tabulated.

There were exceptions, however, in the one arm of the service in which a different condition of command would tell one where to look for them—and a few of these officers are still alive and doing the best of service. But in the main things were as I have described them, and practically the army took its ideas from men who only half understood their subject, and began in the middle, and not at the beginning.

If our cavalry is now inefficient, it is because it tried to arrive at the end without considering the means, and because the teachers did not know what those means really were. Further, since they were keen and anxious to secure commendation, they worked for immediate practical results, which means praise from the inspecting general, and since the inspecting officer generally knew about as much about a horse as he did about a cow, and could only distinguish between fat horses and lean, the harder they worked the more inefficient they became.

The gunners suffered in the same way, and the evil would have been greater in precise proportion to their greater decentralization, for a man working for a purpose will approximate far more nearly to his aim where he has only 150 men and horses, in round numbers, to influence, than when he has to deal directly with 500 of each. Inspecting officers asked for fat horses and they got them, they asked for clean harness and they got that too, and had they required the battery to receive them standing on their heads, they would have got that too.

From time to time, when a gunner or a cavalry man was appointed to a command, things improved a little for the mounted arms, but the infantry suffered. Still, as a rule, it was the infantry that suffered least, for their generals mostly were trained men, and had sufficient ballast of experience to refuse to swallow the new ideas wholesale. They knew there was something wrong about them, though they could not exactly say what, and contented themselves with the tradition of the good old British line, the best thing obtainable till with a true conception of the value of the breech-loader and of the "individual" system of training we can go a step further, and rely on our men fighting equally bravely and enduring losses in single rank at half interval only.

Worse days were in store for us, and from several causes. First came the discontent produced by the abolition of purchase, which filled the messes with dissatisfied men, smarting under a very real grievance. These declared themselves sick of the whole business, took no further interest in their duties, and to everyone who would listen preached the gospel of self-interest only—a good school truly for subalterns to grow up in.

To this was added the habit of idleness, the inevitable outcome of a peacetime long-service system, which habit, being very deeply rooted, simply precluded any hope of obtaining out of men and officers alike the necessary work to make reliable soldiers in the diminished time at their disposal.

Further, under the old system all real responsibility had slipped into the hands of the colonel, the adjutant, and the non-commissioned officers, and when the former became discontented, and the latter ceased to exist, the soil was ready for any noxious weed that might be thrown upon it. Discipline is the essence of the whole thing. Where discipline is, there is contentment; and where there is real contentment, there will be recruits; but the contentment must be real and constant throughout the whole army.

Under a short-service system discipline is impossible without de-centralization of power to the captains, and from that decentralization springs the knowledge necessary for command and staff duties; and eliminating the deficiencies due to the parsimony of the State, for which the soldier is in no way responsible, I believe that had this one change—decentralization of command—accompanied the change to short service, hardly one of the troubles alluded to would ever have arisen.

The Wars of Frederick the Great

The historical section of the General Staff at Berlin has issued the first volume of a series which is to comprise the whole history of the wars of Frederick the Great, and since all the many nations concerned in these campaigns have afforded every facility to the compilers for consulting papers and archives relating to the events, when completed it promises to be an historical work of immense and far wider interest than anything relating to those periods yet produced; and it is very much to be hoped that our own Intelligence Department will take up the translation of it without delay, for the work will be far too bulky for private enterprise, and yet it will—and the first part already does—contain data for the formation of sound tactical opinions of the utmost possible value for all soldiers.

But as this is not likely to happen for some time, I propose to give a tolerably full *précis* of the two introductory chapters relating to the tactics and employment of troops at the commencement of the era, with which the first part will deal—namely, the first Silesian War, 1740-42.

The evolution of the art of war on the conclusion of the Wars of the Spanish Succession had entered on a period of stagnation and partial retrogression. The principles of forms of fighting which had evolved themselves during the wars of Louis XIV. had remained in the main unchanged, but their practical application had lost in energy, and the initiative of the leaders had been sacrificed.

The actual combatant army practically consisted of cavalry and infantry only in the proportions of 1 to 3 in Prussia, 1 to 4 in Austria and her allies, and not quite 1 to 6 in France. The artillery was very weak indeed, only 1 light piece (3-pounder generally) for 1,000 men and a few heavy guns, say 10 to 15,

12- to 24-pounders, as a reserve.

And with a view to maintain unity of direction over the whole, and to develop the fire-power to the utmost, the 'Line' had been evolved.

The tactical unit of the infantry was the battalion in line 4 deep, but in Prussia for fighting purposes only 3 deep, which was divided into sections and divisions which stood side by side without intervals, so that the battalion formed a unit complete in itself. The number of the sections and divisions differed, but was usually 4 of the latter, each of two sections, so that the sections corresponded with our companies; but the division was made on parade with no reference to the actual strength of the "company," which was purely an administrative unit, as it still is in our service. The line was the sole fighting formation: columns were only used for purposes of movement, and of these there were three forms—namely, column of divisions, column of sections, both at wheeling distance, and for short lateral movements a column formed by turning the line, to the right or left, which gave fours or threes. It is curious to notice that just as till quite recently the Prussians recognised two forms of line—namely, 3 deep for manoeuvre and 2 deep for fire—so they then had a 4-deep line for drill purposes, but only used a 3-deep one for firing.

Column of sections was formed from the right only, exactly in the same manner as we still do on the command, "Advance in column from the right." To move to a flank, the companies were wheeled as in "Break into column to the right or left," and this was the ordinary formation; for though the roads were far worse than nowadays, they were mostly much broader, and on approaching a defile the front was reduced by breaking off files, generally from the left, and during the march the distance between the ranks was increased to four paces. To form line from this column to the front, the head changed direction right or left, and continued to advance the full length of the column and then wheeled into line. To form line to a flank they merely wheeled into line in the usual way.

Fire was only delivered by word of command and either by ranks or by sections or divisions. The former was the usual method in all other armies, but the Prussians used only the two latter; but in all, the first rank knelt and the other two locked up. The division or section fire began on the flanks, and worked inwards, and was so regulated that one-half of the battalion always stood with loaded arms at the shoulder, whilst the remainder were loading or firing, and the utmost possible care was given to secure machine-like precision and rapidity in its delivery by ceaseless practice in the firing exercise, thanks to which, after the introduction of the iron ramrod, the Prussian rate of fire reached five rounds a minute—about three times faster than in any other nation. Generally speaking, the attack took place in line, and in order to bring up the battalion as a closed body, it could only advance with small and slow steps, the pace of 28 inches and the cadence 75 to 80; but marching in step was as yet unknown, though they did march in time to the beat of the drum, increasing or diminishing the rate as indicated by the instrument.

> The great difficulty of the time was to combine fire and movement, for only under these circumstances did the attack become possible, but in most armies the want of adequate peace-training placed most insuperable difficulties in the way. As a rule, the attack came to a stand after passing through the zone of the artillery fire and entering that of the musketry; the losses then soon brought the assailants to a halt; then ensued, either with or without word of command, a stationary fire-fight. After this halt lasted a time, the officers either did or did not succeed in stopping it and forcing the line forward with the bayonet.

Of course there was no want of suggestions as to how to secure the desired end. Some generals believed it possible to push straight in with the bayonet without firing at all, and amongst these was no less a person than Maurice de Saxe, who says in his *Reveries*:

> The firearm is not so terrible as one thinks; few men are killed in action by fire from the front. I have seen volleys that did not hit four men, and neither I nor anyone else saw an effect sufficient to have prevented us from continuing our advance and revenging ourselves with the bayonet and pursuing fire.

All, however, agreed in the importance of postponing the halt to fire as long as possible, and then keeping it strictly under control.

The Austrians covered their advance by their grenadier companies, who were employed entirely as our old skirmishers, halting, firing, loading, and running forward, whilst the closed battalion followed in rear without checking. If the attack failed, then, whilst retreating, named flies had to halt, front, fire, and regain their places in the ranks. This was the general method of fighting in use in all countries, and if

ATTACK OF PRUSSIAN INFANTRY

One of Schill's followers

the Prussians succeeded therein in excelling all their competitors, this was due to their better peacetime training, and to their truer comprehension of the spirit of the game, which led them to attach greater importance to increasing the development of fire, its utilization in the attack, and the maintenance of unquestioning discipline in all movements. Their three-deep formation gave them a marked advantage in development of front, and the march in step (which they had been the first to introduce) gave them an additional means of securing order and accuracy in their movements.

The fire in attacking was thus regulated. The battalion advanced in line, with bands playing and drums beating. On the command of fire being given, the music ceased, and the portions designated to commence firing halted and made ready, then advanced three long steps, whilst the rest of the line continued to move at the ordinary pace. At the third pace the front rank dropped on the knee, and the two rear rank ones locked up, the volley was delivered, and the body regained its place in the line, loading on the march.

Thus the whole line during the firing of the different portions remained in constant though slow motion, and ceaseless practice as well as the iron discipline in which the troops were trained guaranteed that even in the sharpest fire the movement would be carried out with the regularity of machinery.

The cavalry of the line was organised in *cuirassiers*, *carbineers*, and dragoons. As the value of infantry had been so much increased by the introduction of firearms, it was hoped to secure the same improvement in the mounted forces by arming them with the carbine and devoting equal attention to their training in its use. But the idea was overdone, and the true spirit of the arm suffered in consequence. This was more the case in Prussia than in Austria, in which country the true cavalry spirit, with which Prince Eugene had inspired his regiments, protected them from a similar misapprehension of their duties.

The squadron was everywhere the tactical unit, formed in three ranks, and subdivided into "troops," in Prussia into four as at present. Line was re-formed by wheeling from column as described above for the infantry. On the march along the roads open column of troops was the normal formation, but across country they often moved on a squadron front. The execution of the charge varied in different armies.

In Prussia the regulations of 1727 laid down:

> All squadrons shall advance to the attack with swords at the engage, standards flying, and trumpets sounding, and every commander is held bound, on his honour and reputation, to allow no shooting, but always to ride home with the sword.

> When squadrons attack, they are to move at the trot, and never to wait to be attacked, but always charge first.

But at the period of the first Silesian War these regulations were by no means always attended to. In advancing cavalry against cavalry, they generally went straight at each other without manoeuvring, sending some skirmishers out from the flanks of the squadrons to prepare the attack by their fire. There was little scope for manoeuvring, for the half-column was still unknown, and the line to the front, by squadrons moving up by the shortest way, as practiced nowadays, was also of subsequent invention; and further, the troops were not sufficiently drilled in close bodies, and in jumping obstacles, etc.

In Austria there were two kinds of attack practiced—one employed against the Turks, the other against Christians; in the latter case the squadrons advanced, with swords hanging from the wrist and pistols in hand, in two ranks. On approaching the adversary the gallop was sounded, the pistols fired in his face at 20 paces, and then the attack ridden home at the fullest speed of the horses, the men being further instructed to hit the horses of the enemy on the head, as "this always has good effect." Against the Turks, however, they moved in three ranks, slowly and well closed up, in order to halt in good order and deliver volleys, so great was the terror which these consummate horsemen and their sharp swords had inspired in the Christian ranks.

If the enemy was defeated, a portion pursued whilst the rest rallied; but rallying was so little practiced that after a charge the troops generally got out of hand. "Against infantry their tactics were the same, and, as a rule, the result of such charges delivered at a trot or moderate canter was often a failure," as might be expected; whereas the Turks, charging home recklessly at full gallop, usually sabered everything they came across, and were so much feared that the infantry took *chevaux-de-frise* connected together with chains into the field with them, and whenever they halted, put up this obstacle in front to protect them.

All line cavalry were trained for dismounted work, particularly the dragoons, who fought like an infantry battalion. Dismounted cavalry were also much employed in the defence of localities.

The French adhered to this line of action the longest, whilst in Austria and Germany the tendency to dismounted fighting gradually disappeared. The hussars held a middle place between the line cavalry and the irregulars, and fought mostly as skirmishers. Their leading sections engaged the enemy in front with fire, whilst the remainder followed close behind the flanks, to be subsequently extended against the enemy's flanks. If charged, they gave way and sought shelter behind the line cavalry. The irregulars fought partly on foot and partly mounted, much after the manner of hussars, but without closed reserves, and generally with less approach to order.

On foot each man fought as a skirmisher for his own hand. In a battle they were chiefly employed on the flanks and in difficult ground, which protected them from the volleys and closed attacks of the regular infantry. The Austrians had in this respect a great advantage over the Prussians, and made the most of it, but the want of discipline and love of plunder which characterized these hordes often proved a serious trouble to their own side, particularly when fighting in their own country.

Up to the beginning of the first Silesian War, the artillery had no tactical training to speak of. The men were trained to serve their guns, to prepare ammunition, and in the construction of batteries, and in Prussia they had an annual course of fourteen days' target practice. But no artillery regulations existed, and special orders were necessary on each occasion to put together groups or batteries. The light artillery, 3-, 4-, and 6-pounders, with an effective range of 1,500 yards, were allotted by pairs to the battalions, and the heavy 8-, 12-, and 24-pounders with howitzers were united in large batteries and employed in the line of battle at suitable places.

In the attack, after a short period of preparatory fire, the heavy guns were brought up to case-shot range, about 500 yards, and the battalion guns sought to get in to 200 or 300 yards before opening fire, and were dragged up by hand, and in advance of the battalion intervals till the infantry firing began. In defence, the guns were placed somewhat in advance of the infantry line and on its flanks, and where possible the heavy guns were grouped together in positions from which they could bring a fire to bear on the advancing enemy's flank, and when time permitted they were protected by earthworks and obstacles.

The position of the three arms relatively to one another was laid down in the *Order of Battle*, a document which had to be specially prepared for each campaign or minor undertaking. The desire to develop to the utmost possible pitch the firepower of the infantry had led to the diminution of depth with extreme extension of front, the first being made as strong as possible at the expense of the second, and the third line was very rarely seen at all. The cavalry were placed on the flanks, both to protect these and also to secure a free field of action. The artillery found no place in the formal order of battle, but, as above mentioned, orders had to be issued for its employment on each special occasion.

The army was further divided into wings, each under a special commander, but these commanders had no separate power of their own. The leading idea was to bring the army into action as a whole, and this intention was further indicated by drawing up the battalions of the first line at equal intervals of 20 paces throughout the line, no special intervals marking the limit of the wing or brigade commands, the sole duty of the leaders of these subdivisions being limited to maintaining the direction ordered, the closing of gaps, and the timely support of any portion of the line that might happen to be driven in." (It does not, however, appear how this last duty was to be performed, for the brigade and regimental commands stood side by side, and not one behind the other, so only the wing commander would appear to have had the power of ordering up a battalion or any portion of the second line to the support of the first line.) "The second line followed the first at 300 paces' distance as a rule. This distance being fixed so that it should not suffer from the fire aimed at the first one.

The sections devoted to the arrangement of encampments and the different orders of march are hardly of sufficient general interest for reproduction here. It will be enough to call attention to the extreme formality of all proceedings which followed as a necessity from the prevailing conditions of enlistment and culture of the people generally, and the sparse-population of the districts in which the fighting mostly took place. As soldiering was unpopular, desertion was rife, and hence it would have been impossible to quarter the soldiers in towns and villages, even had such cover existed in sufficient quantity. As the trained soldier represented a considerable sum of money, he was too valuable to be exposed to the chance of sickness which bivouacs would have entailed, and hence the necessity of tents; and the general ignorance of troopers and the absence of reliable maps, more perhaps the want of newspapers, rendered it a matter of extreme difficulty to get full and reliable information of the enemy's movements, and hence the necessity of camping in order of battle ready to turn out and fight at short notice.

Tactics of the Opposing Forces Before the First Silesian War

In a previous letter I gave a *précis* of the tactics of the Prussian, Austrian, and French armies as they were before the commencement of the first Silesian War—*i. e.*, before the great genius of Frederick had been brought to bear on the subject; and for the details of the condition or tactics of the three arms separately, I must refer to the former article. In the following lines I follow the German General Staff account of how the three arms were employed in battle, and the general ideas of how war was conducted in those days.

When a battle was imminent, as a rule the general of the attacking side rode out with the advance guard, in order personally to see with his own eyes where and how his enemy was drawn up, and thereby to regulate the approach and formation of his own forces. As in those days he could, approach to a distance at which all details were clearly visible, it will be evident what a wide difference there is between his position then and now, when, owing to the increased range of all arms, and still more to the enormous increase in the numbers engaged, he is compelled to base his plans on the reports conveyed to him by others, frequently emanating from private soldiers who in the first engagements, at any rate of the next war, can only know what the manoeuvres have taught them, and hence the extreme importance of making these as like the real thing as possible is apparent.

Thus at Blenheim, Eugene and Marlborough preceded their army with 40 squadrons taken from both wings. The consultation as to the manner of attack and the issue of the necessary orders occupied about an hour, during which the army ap-

DUKE OF MARLBOROUGH AT RAMILLIES

RAMILLIES – THE CAVALRY CHARGE UNDER MARLBOROUGH

proached and halted at a distance from the enemy of about a mile.

The formation of the lines then followed. The heads of the columns wheeled to either flank, marched forward their own length, and then wheeled into line. Owing to the low degree of skill in manoeuvring that these generally possessed, this operation took considerable time, and when completed, the advance guard fell, back into its place as assigned to it in the normal order of battle, unless meanwhile some special mission was entrusted to it.

The artillery was now brought up to the front and endeavoured to silence the enemy's guns, whilst the line remained halted out of their range. After this fire had lasted an hour or so, the army moved slowly forward to the attack, halting now and again to correct their order and direction. The cavalry kept its place throughout this movement on the flanks till within 500 or 600 yards of the enemy, when they rode forward and engaged the enemy. This slow advance and the constant halts within effective range of the enemy's artillery was an exceedingly trying ordeal for the cavalry, and demanded a very high order of discipline, and as a consequence its leaders were always inclined to curtail the period as much as possible and attack at the earliest opportunity; and whether such attacks—of which there are many examples—were actually due to impatience of loss, or to a truer conception of the duties of cavalry, in either case the book tacticians of those days seriously blamed them.

If their charge were successful, then theoretically only a few squadrons were to pursue the beaten horsemen, but the bulk were to wheel in and fall on the flanks and rear of the infantry. Practically it generally happened that after an obstinate hand-to-hand fight, the victors stuck to the defeated cavalry and together drifted away from the battlefield, not returning to it for the rest of the day.

During this cavalry fight, the advancing line of infantry had entered the zone of musketry fire, and now came the real tussle.

Even in those days however much as leaders desired it practically, it was not possible to close with the bayonet without firing, the attacking line halted and a fire-fight ensued—if the first line alone could not establish a fair superiority, it was the duty of the second to come up and carry it on. But it will be obvious what an advantage a highly trained infantry such as the Prussian, whose rate of volley firing was three times that of its opponents, must have had in such a struggle, "and the superiority once obtained, the advance with the bayonet followed as a matter of course." There was, therefore, no essential difference of principle between the infantry fight of those days and the present, only the struggle for fire superiority takes place within 700 yards now instead of within 200 then, and the magazine fire at 300 has practically taken the place of cold steel.

The difference in the detail of execution other than that due to distance is, that since nowadays the rate of fire is everywhere equal, as far as the infantry alone are concerned, the superiority can only be obtained by higher discipline ensuring more accurate fire and its concentration on portions of the enemy's line only. It will be obvious, too, how great the retrogression was when the column was reintroduced for attack purposes, whereby the defender was able to concentrate his fire on fractions of the assailant's force only, and not *vice versa*: but where both defenders and attackers start equal as regards discipline, it will be evident that only the previous employment of the artillery by the latter can give them the requisite guarantee of success, though the power the initiative gives to the assailant of concentrating masses against a line equally strong and equally weak everywhere still leaves a balance in favour of the attacking side.

> If the enemy's first line was overthrown, then the order of the attacking line was re-established and operations commenced against his second one, and this process was repeated till at last the enemy took to flight in disorder, when any fresh troops at hand were sent in pursuit; but, as a rule, pursuits were not instituted, the victors re-formed on the conquered ground and advanced a short distance. The rallying took so much time, and the advance in these ponderous lines was so slow, that generally all touch of the beaten army was lost, and it was left free to continue its retreat unmolested. Cavalry was rarely used in pursuits, and in fact they (*i. e.* pursuits) were generally looked on with disfavour.

The conduct of the defenders generally depended on the result of the above mentioned introductory cavalry fight. If the assailants were overthrown, then it frequently happened that their infantry renounced the offensive, and this very partial result was in those days accounted as a victory. If, on the other hand, the defenders' cavalry were beaten, the battle was yet not lost to them, more particularly if the flanks rested on a substantial obstacle. The first line received the enemy with its fire, and the second protected the rear of the former against the returning cavalry, and if the first line was penetrated, the battalions nearest at hand in the second advanced against the assailants who had got through, with the bayonet.

If their efforts failed, then the battle was lost, for adequate reserves were rarely provided, and it was impracticable to move one part of either line without compromising the whole. If they succeeded in repelling the attack by lire, then it was the custom to rest contented with the result obtained—counter-attacks were rarely attempted, pursuits still more seldom—for one was afraid of relinquishing the substantial advantages of a selected position, or of risking the carefully arranged order of battle for doubtful results.

Defence, therefore, was confined to the maintenance of a line once selected; the conception of a sectional defence, or of the offensive-defensive, had scarcely developed itself.

In case retreat became unavoidable, the first line retired through the intervals of the second, which had to resist until the first had again selected and occupied a position in order to take up and cover the second, when it in turn fell back, the same course being also followed by the cavalry. If the retreat took place in disorder, then all alike made the best time they could back to the next defensible section of the ground, and in view of the cautious timidity of the assailant, its occupation generally put a stop to the pursuit.

Taken all in all, the battles of this epoch were mostly of the "parallel" order, in which both sides mutually wear one another out, in purely frontal attacks, and the side which could boast of the greatest endurance and courage, together with the best discipline, ultimately conquered. Occasionally the timely cooperation of a turning column turned the scale, but more frequently the idea was to "surprise" victory, by attacking an enemy whilst passing a defile, rather than by directing the strength of an army against its adversary's weakness to "compel" victory.

Great leaders, such as Prince Eugene and Marlborough,[1] fully understood both courses, but in long successions of battles in Louis XIV.'s time they stood alone in their art and tactical genius. The others

---

1. *Marlborough's Wars* Volume 1—1702-1707 & Volume 2—1707-1709 by Frank Taylor also published by Leonaur.

adhered more and more, as time went on, to the hard-and-fast rules of the game—a proceeding which, in case of disaster, relieved them of personal responsibility.

Thus the tactical science of the epoch had on the whole evolved the form best suited to the characteristics of armies of the period and their weapons—namely, the closed line as principal supporter of the fire-fight, but the form had tended towards solidification, and showed itself rigid and incapable of adaptation to circumstances. A false conception of the condition on which success depended had led the minds of tacticians of the day astray in a search after the unattainable—namely, a normal form of action equally adaptable to all conditions. What in the hands of the masters was 'art' in the highest form, in the hands of their disciples became pure 'rule of thumb'—a characteristic tendency of the time which will be found to repeat itself also in the strategy of the same period.

And if one were writing a history of the tactical decadence in the England of the present day, the position could not be summed up in truer or terser terms.

The strategy or method of conducting war—(apart from the influence of the personality of the leaders and the mental evolution of the troops, the method of conducting war in all periods)—is conditioned by the politics, the system of supply, the roads or other lines of communication, and the recruiting and tactics of the armies employed.

The political circumstances of the Louis XIV. period led to the formation of numerous coalitions, held together by their momentary common interests, and as these varied, the elements of the coalition also varied; nations fighting one campaign on one side the next on the other, according as they thought to perceive that their interest lay. Further, besides the interests of the State, a number of other personal considerations had to be taken into account. Dynastic interests, unworthy passions of rulers and their favourites, intrigues in the court parties on either side, sometimes played a decisive part. Thus alliances were lightly entered into, and as lightly broken. Further, diplomacy exercised its influence not only in the stages of operations preceding actual contact, but even made itself felt in the field itself.

The result was to weaken the energy with which military operations were conducted. The constant consideration for the wishes of the allies, the striving to induce the enemy's allies to change sides, the fear lest neutral parties should join in—all led to the result that the combatants rarely put out their full fighting strength. To destroy the enemy and compel him to accept peace at any price, ceased to be the leading idea: on the contrary, the highest art lay in entangling him diplomatically; and at last it came to this, that war was only carried on nominally; and a further consequence was, that almost every treaty of peace contained in itself the seed of fresh discussions.

By the side of politics, the method of supply also had its influence. In the Thirty Years' War[2] armies had lived exclusively on requisitions, and in doing so had proceeded to such excesses that war meant utter desolation to the tract wherein it was waged. In the following period, as a reaction, an altogether exaggerated idea of the rights of private property prevailed; at the same time, the custom of always marching and camping the armies concentrated as a whole brought more men together on the same ground than the resources of the farms and villages in the vicinity could suffice to supply.

One was, therefore, compelled to provide for the troops out of one's own means, and therefore, in advancing, to drag supplies after one; only forage for the horses was obtained on the spot, or brought in by foraging parties, for, with the very considerable numbers of cavalry, sufficient wagon-trains were not available. Hence magazines and bakeries had to be provided, and these magazines had to be moved up step by step with the progress of the armies. If the magazine system broke down, nothing was left but supply by requisitions, which, for reasons above given, rarely sufficed; and since in those days irregularity in the feeding of troops led to desertion *en masse*, supply played an altogether disproportionate part in the regulation of the marches to what it does nowadays in European warfare."

The condition and nature of the roads by which the supplies were brought up and the troops moved must also be borne in recollection.

These appear to have been very similar to those in Scotland which gave rise to the well-known lines: *Had you seen these roads before they*

---

2. *The Thirty Years' War* by Samuel R. Gardiner also published by Leonaur.

were made, You would lift up your hands and bless General Wade.

The post-roads were generally some 11 yards in width, and mostly of the same nature as the surrounding country, from which they were frequently not even marked off by ditches or rows of trees. To keep them in order was the duty of the land-owners through whose estates they passed, and they usually confined themselves to pitching down an occasional cart-load of stones, or throwing in a few faggots of brushwood when the state of things got too bad, but no supervision existed to see that even this was done; only, if things were very bad, the travel-ler had a right to diverge into the fields and turn the obstacle as best he could.

The construction of the great high-roads was only taken in hand during the second half of the eighteenth century, but was then rapidly proceeded with, so that Napoleon found ready to his hand a widespread net-work of well-constructed roads, which alone rendered much of his strategy possible. Things were, of course, much more favourable when great rivers were available as lines of communication, and hence the importance attached to operating, where possible, along the valleys of such rivers as the Danube, the Po, the Rhine, etc.,—an importance which, long after the conditions have changed against them, still leads to misconception sometimes as to their value.

I have purposely extracted much on this head to mark specially the importance the Prussian Staff attach to these conditions as modifying the method of making war, and because also existing conditions in India are so very similar yet in many parts of the country, and hence explain much which in the eyes of Staff College pundits appears to be antiquated in our Indian methods, and the following lines will bring out even more clearly the influence that the method of recruiting and raising our Indian Army must also necessarily exercise.

As regards the influence that recruiting and completion of the armies had on their employment, it must be borne in mind that the standing armies of this period were on the whole bodies of men entirely detached from the civilian population, always ready for the war purposes of their king. The Prussian Army had carried out this idea further to its logical conclusion than any other, and alone was independent of militia drafts to com-plete it to a war footing.

But the difficulty was to supply the losses caused by war, by trained men, and the immense expense of maintenance in peace.

Each trained man in fact represented so much capital, and considerations of economy therefore modified the daring of the leaders, and also tended to an excess of caution in tactics, and led to an excessive value being attached to the defensive and the use of entrenchments—a tendency equally apparent in the British Army of today.

All these influences exercised a retarding effect on the plans of campaign, which, as a rule, were not worked out by the commander-in-chief destined to execute them, but by the diplomatists, who sought to draft them in such a manner that the private interests of allies were equally well protected, and this naturally led to a dispersion of force all over the frontiers, instead of its concentration on the decisive point.

It will be evident, therefore, how great the advantage was when the king in person drew up his own plans and carried them into execution, and still more so when, as in the case of Napoleon, the conditions of the country placed him at the head of a nation in arms and rendered him indifferent to the expenditure of human life. It is principally because these very essential facts in the evolutions of war have been overlooked by our English strategists, notably Hamley, that their teaching is so entirely barren and misleading.

These diplomatic negotiations frequently dragged on for months, so that the best opportunity for action was often allowed to slip. . . . . . When at last the contracting parties were agreed as to their several shares in the coming campaign, then each court drew up its own plan of operations, in which the general-in-chief might or might not be consulted, but on whom no real responsibility rested; and when this was finally entrusted into his hands for execution, it was practically never omitted to caution him specially to take the utmost care not to risk his expensive army, and in all cases of difficulty to call in his subordinates for council.

It is obvious what difficulties such a method of procedure entailed and how inevitably the energy of the war was crippled; and only occasionally we find men of exceptional ability, such as Marlborough and Prince Eugene, with here and there momentarily a marshal of France, breaking the bonds that held them, and acquiring a certain degree of respect for their own individuality.

As a rule, the objective of the campaign was a province or frontier fortress, never the enemy's field army, a point again on which almost the whole of Hamley's 'Strategy' turns;[3] and this being settled, the next thing was to accumulate the magazines on which to base the movement. Then followed the march into the enemy's country, which, owing to bad roads and the enormous train, frequently was of extreme slowness. Ten English miles a day was considered exceptional, and often four to five was a fair average performance.

When the assailant had thus penetrated a few miles into the enemy's country, generally to some previously agreed on line of defence, a halt had to be made to bring up the bakeries and magazines, and these had then to be protected by detachments; and since no organised *'etappen'* (*i. e.*, line of communication troops) existed, the advancing army rapidly became weaker, and when the enemy was at last reached, it was only considered advisable to attack if the latter was evidently surprised in his concentration; otherwise manoeuvring was resorted to.

Even when a battle had been risked and won, the destruction of the enemy's field army was far from being attained, for, ow-

---

3. Hamley's failure to appreciate the paramount importance of making the enemy's main army the objective in military operations is so marked, that at the U. S. Infantry and Cavalry School, where Hamley's *Operations of War* was, until recently, used as a text-book, it was deemed advisable to supplement the text with a series of questions and answers, of which the following was the most important, and was given the greatest possible emphasis:

What should always be the object of military operations? *To Defeat the Main Army of the Enemy.* As a preliminary, the occupation of territory, or the seizure of a strategic point, may be necessary operations, but *these must be regarded as merely incidental to the one great object of meeting and decisively beating the enemy's principal force.*

Hamley's oversight in this respect does not seem so remarkable, however, when we reflect that from the passing of Napoleon to the advent of Grant, no commander seems to have appreciated this great, though simple, military truth. From the beginning of the War of Secession until Grant assumed command of the Union armies, the Federal operations in Virginia seem to have had for their paramount object the capture of Richmond; but Grant recognized the fact that his true objective was *Lee's army,* and grappling with his adversary at the Wilderness, he held fast to him with a grip that nothing could relax until the surrender at Appomattox. So, too. Von Moltke ever acted upon the principle that no geographical or other consideration could modify the fact that his true objective was the enemy's main army.—A. L. W,.

ing to want of energy in the pursuit, the adversary had generally ample opportunity to recover himself, and then reappeared on the theatre of war again, and not without good prospect of results, for the attacking party had meanwhile probably turned itself against the frontier fortifications.

The system of defence was on a par with that of the attack. As a rule, all available troops (*i.e.*, available after a host of points of secondary importance had been, attended to) were united in a central defensive position, where they awaited the attack, and if manoeuvred out of it, then they fell back to another.

To these positions great importance was attached, and they were previously reconnoitred, and often fortified provisionally on a large scale in war; but it is fair to say that several of the best men were strongly against them and pointed out the drawbacks inherent in them.

Not more successfully, on the whole, than others have been in a similar undertaking in England of late years, where the exaggerated idea of the fire-power of the defensive attributed to the new arms, and the general ignorance of all sound principles in war, still lead from time to time to equally unsound proposals, such as the defence of London, by *Provisional* fortifications.

From all the aforesaid reasons, the chief characteristics of the wars of those days were 'positions and manoeuvres,' avoiding as far as possible the decision of battle.

And, as a rule, the attack usually did come to a stand before these defences, for the fire-power was already sufficient to make the success of a direct assault pretty uncertain, more especially owing to the absence of a sufficient artillery power to prepare the way.

The assailant then deployed opposite to the defender, and formally 'offered him battle,' an offer not often accepted; or, if the roads permitted, sought to frighten him out of his position by threatening a flank. If neither succeeded, then both sides entrenched themselves and endeavoured to starve each other out, or to induce each other by diversions to disperse their force, and then attack before these could be called in again.

But generally the tendency was to avoid fighting; the destruction of the enemy's field army was not the object of the war, only the occupation of a province or fortress, and manoeuvres sufficed for the attainment of this without incurring the risk of a battle.

Many reasons gave an apparent justification of these views: first of these was the necessity of economizing the troops. Battles, owing to the tactics of the day, were very bloody, and the losses very difficult to replace; and further, the issue of a fight depended more on chance than in the present day, owing to the want of adaptability to circumstances in the troops themselves, due to deficient military education, and still more often to the petty jealousies of the subordinate leaders. The results of a battle were also too small, owing to the tardiness of pursuit rendered necessary both by the tactics and conditions of supply; and finally, whilst all the glory of a successful manoeuvre belonged of right to the leader, the credit of a victorious battle fell to the troops almost entirely, the leader being liable to blame for sacrificing his men.

The above does not pretend to be a verbal translation of the whole of the chapter referred to—space alone would utterly forbid the attempt; but I think it gives all the main points, and more especially the spirit of the original. The point I wish to notice is the influence which this old-fashioned school of thought has had on the evolution of existing conceptions of strategy, more especially in our own service. It was from the writers of those days that Frederick's generals, and the bulk of his officers who studied at all, derived their ideas—and though he himself broke with the system as far as his conditions allowed him, and was never afraid to trust all to the decision of the battle, yet his absorption of all duties in himself, and habit of keeping his instructions secret, accessible only to the few and not to the army at large, resulted on his death in the resurrection of the old ideas; and thus when the Revolution broke out, and the armed nation it produced gave Napoleon a weapon such as no other general in Europe could boast of, the Prussians were in as unfavourable a position to encounter him as the rest of the powers, who had had no Frederick to boast of.

What need for wonder, therefore, at his astounding successes? But the evil of these mistaken notions did not die here. Writers, not soldiers, then attempted to explain Napoleon's and Frederick's victories in conformity with the old traditions, and this was more especially the case in France, from whom, again, we have always borrowed most largely.

There is an excuse for this retrogression, more especially in our case, for, except in Prussia, during the long peace, the idea of the standing army was everywhere revived, and with it came the need of economy of lives in battle, which gives a specious appearance of correctness to the idea of manoeuvring, as against fighting, strategy, and which also prepared the way for the ready acceptance of the doctrine that the chief object of the training of troops for war is to teach them how to avoid getting killed, and not how to kill, a doctrine which (to our shame be it said) appears at the present moment to be more widely held in England than in any other country in Europe, though it is so diametrically opposed to our national tendencies.

The main difference between the conditions then and now which wants to be brought home to the public, more particularly as regards England and possible European war, is, that whereas in those days three things were necessary for success, "money," "money," and "more money," for money could buy men, as we know from experience: now it is "men," "money," and "more men," for though money is necessary for armament and supply, it can no longer buy men.

But the whole conception of modern war is based on a ruthless expenditure of life to gain certain ends, quite as much on the line of march, and indeed more so, than in the field, for there skilful massing at the right place and time, the mutual support of the three arms, and a training in discipline in peace so thorough that troops can be counted on to face even the heaviest losses when ordered to, still enable great results to be obtained with a small total expenditure of men, though locally the losses may amount to annihilation; but to ensure the arrival of the men at the right time and places may entail losses on the line of march far exceeding in the aggregate those incurred in the field. This utter ruthlessness with regard to the suffering of the individual was the true mainspring of Napoleonic strategy, and alone rendered his battle policy possible. Frederick and Wellington were both too much hampered by the money value of their soldiers to dare to emulate his feats in this respect. It may be as well to give some figures in support of this, for it is a point not touched on by our text-book writers, my authority being Clausewitz, Book V., Chapter 12.

Napoleon crossed the Niemen in 1812 with 301,00 men on the 24th of June. Before he reached Smolensk, the 15th of August, he had lost 95,500 on the march alone. Three weeks later, before Borodino, he had lost in all 144,000 men (including killed in action), and eight days later 198,000 men. For the first period the daily loss was l-150th of the whole; in the. second, l-120th; and in third, 1-19th.

Allowing 60,000 for losses due to the enemy's fire, those on the march are still more than 2 to 1.

All this, it may be objected, is, after all, ancient history; but at the present moment, when it seems as if a last desperate attempt to re-introduce long service were about to be made, it is well to bring the matter to the front, for long service would mean the resuscitation of these old and effete theories, and as a consequence we could have no hope of success in any conflict with a European army. One last point remains to be noticed in this connection. A long-service war-trained army, trained in the school of Victory, as was the old Peninsular Army, is undeniably the most perfect fighting machine conceivable; but a long-service peacetime army tends inevitably to over-centralization, the stereotyping of forms, and the utter decay of military knowledge.

Idleness and *ennui* in its officers and their divorce from their men is its certain consequence, and it is to such conditions prevailing in the Home Army during the peace after Waterloo that we owe the low level of military intelligence, and the total want of sound principle in our staff and our educational institutions. Work, constant, ceaseless work, is the sole guarantee for the maintenance of fighting efficiency; but men are only human, and when no obvious reason for such work exists, as was the case in a good old long-service battalion, requiring perhaps only 20 recruits a year, it is utterly hopeless to expect such exertion.

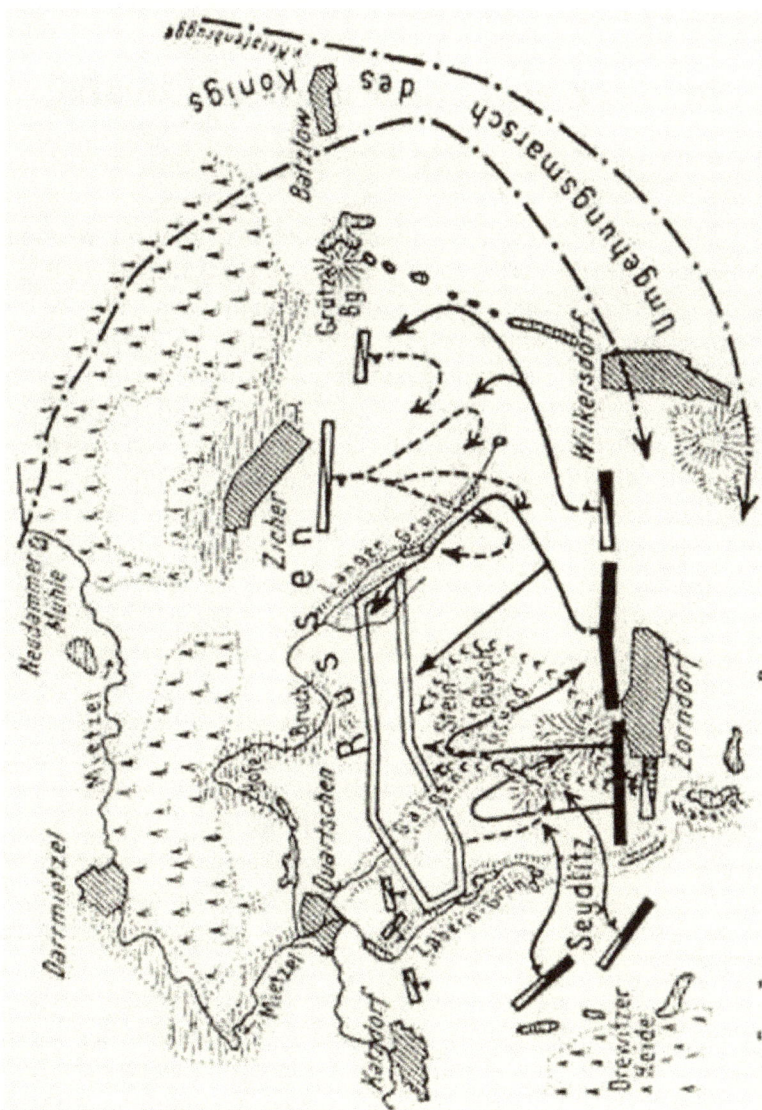

Seydlitz and the Prussian Cavalry

There has been much discussion of late as to the true position and employment of cavalry in large bodies on the battlefield. In England the current of opinion has set very strongly against the cavalry the usual line of argument being that if at Waterloo the Napoleonic cavalry failed to effect anything against our squares, armed only with the muzzle-loader, what prospect of success can any horsemen of to-day have against troops armed with the more perfect weapons of the present day; and the failure of the French, Austrian, and Prussian cavalry against the breech-loaders is quoted in confirmation of these views, whilst the true significance of the successes of the latter against the old imperial army of France is minimized or ignored altogether.

The true answer to these views is, that the Napoleonic cavalry was most inferior; how inferior I have endeavoured to show in a previous article. And as a consequence of the tendency after the close of the Napoleonic period to exalt the excellence of everything French which existed at the time, both in England and the Continent, French conclusions were accepted wholesale, and everywhere the cavalry were trained to distrust themselves; and hence it was no wonder if, as weapons improved and, the teaching of experience became more and more remote, there were wanting men with confidence enough in their arm to lead it in such a manner as to afford it a prospect of success.

The real cause of surprise is, that under the circumstances the cavalry succeeded in going so near to success as it actually did—how near, I have endeavoured to show in an article on *Cavalry on the Battlefield,* in the first series of letters published under the same title as these. That article was written about 1883-4, and since then I have found an immense amount of evidence to confirm my views in the pages of Prince Hohenlohe's *Gesprache fiber Kavallerie,* and in Hoenig's *Die*

Kavallerie Division als Schlachten Korper (translated by Captain Lever-son, R.E., in the *Journal of the R. C. S I.*) and his subsequent works, one of which, *Tactical Guides for the Formation and Leading of a Cavalry Division*, is now also appearing in the *United Service Magazine*, thanks to the zeal of the same author.

The chief obstacles I have found to the acceptance of these views are the extraordinary ignorance that prevails as to the history of tactics before Napoleon's time, and the growing tendency to assume that the nature of war has so completely changed since the introduction of the breech-loader that it is mere waste of time to study anything that went before. Of the two, I consider the latter the most dangerous error, for the conditions of armament and composition of the troops were too dissimilar and the duration of the campaign too short to admit of the deduction of true guiding principles for any arm.

The origin of modern tactics dates from the time when it was first distinctly recognized that "fire alone decides" as regards infantry *versus* infantry, and that "cavalry must rely on their swords alone and the speed of their horses when thoroughly extended." Both these principles were thoroughly admitted at the commencement of the Seven Years' War. The next step in the evolution of the three arms was the development of the power of artillery, when acting in conjunction with troops otherwise not particularly reliable, and this was the chief teaching of Napoleon's battlefields. Since then the balance between the three arms has been so often upset by the progress of invention that the key to the teaching of the many wars which have occurred since 1815 can only be found by those who have followed the development of each arm through its successive stages.

I believe that the discredit into which cavalry on the battlefield have fallen, more particularly during the last twenty-five years, (as at time of first publication), is due almost entirely to the acceptance of the French dogma that cavalry cannot charge unshaken infantry. Certainly the failure of the French cavalry against our own squares at Waterloo may seem to confirm this view, and it would do so if the word "cavalry" always represented a fixed standard of excellence, but that is not the case.

On the contrary, probably no word has ever been used to describe things so widely differing in merit as the men on horses of Napoleon's day and the cavalry of Frederick. I referred above to our own squares at Waterloo, but it would be better for my line of argument to fix one's attention on the Prussian infantry only, for by so doing we eliminate

CAVALRY SQUARES AT WATERLOO

the variable conditions of nationality and armament, for the Prussian infantry from 1813-15 were armed with the very same muskets that their fathers had carried before them under Frederick, and time had presumably not improved them, and the men who carried them could not in discipline and training have been anywhere nearly on a par with the troops who fought out the Seven Years' War, who again were very fairly matched by their enemies, the Austrians and Russians. If, therefore, these latter were in almost every instance ridden over by the Prussian cavalry, it follows that the French cavalry, who subsequently failed to break Prussian, Austrian, and Russian squares, must have been very inferior indeed.

In an article I wrote last summer, entitled *The Napoleonic Cavalry*, I described what these latter were at considerable length, and therefore need not go over the ground a second time. I propose now to show in detail what the Prussians actually were capable of only sixty years before, and leave it to my readers to decide which of the two it would be best for us to take as a model. My authority is Graf von Bismarck,, who, if not, strictly speaking, a contemporary of the events, lived near enough to the times to obtain his information at first hand from the actors in the scenes he describes. The particular work from which I quote is *Seydlitz, and the Prussian Cavalry under Frederick the Great*, and those sufficiently interested in the matter will find a great deal of valuable detail about his life in Varnhagen von Ense's biography, which is, however, too detailed for my present purpose.

About Seydlitz's early life, it is sufficient to mention that he was a consummate rider and swordsman, and trained his own squadron on the principle of doing everything he asked of his subordinates as well as, and better than, they could—an ideal principle not often attained. Roszbach, 5th November, 1757, was the first occasion on which he held an independent cavalry command, and he used the opportunity to such good effect that it will forever remain as an example of what cavalry could do under the old conditions. And apart from those due to the infantry armament, he was much hampered by existing regulations for the cavalry itself.

The individual training of men and horses had reached already a very high degree of perfection, and the squadrons in themselves appear to have been well in the hands of their leaders, but their collective movements were still slow, as all movements had to be made "to the halt." The precise date when forming on the move was introduced I have been unable to ascertain, though it appears to me to have been somewhere within the following three years.

The odds against the Prussians were overwhelming—namely, 16,000 infantry and 5,400 cavalry in forty-five squadrons against a total of ninety battalions and eighty-four squadrons, making 64,000 men in all, who on the 4th of November lay in such a strong position that Frederick did not think it wise to attack it, and retired to a position some five miles away, where he pitched his camp on the top of a low ridge in sight of the enemy. The morning of the 5th was passed in skirmishing between the hussars and the light troops of both sides. Shortly after 9 a. m. the French set the bulk of their forces in march in two columns, directed well clear of the Prussian left flank, apparently with the object of cutting their line of retreat.

This was clearly seen and reported to the king, who, however, refused or pretended not to believe that the movement signified anything important. He ordered the men to have their dinners, and sat down to his own, to which most of his generals had been invited, and, having finished it, ascended a tower in the village of Roszbach to see with his own eyes what was going on. The enemy had by this time reached the prolongation of the Prussian line with their infantry, and their cavalry and artillery were some distance further to the front, heading for a little knoll, the "Janus Hill," which lay some 4,000 yards behind the Prussian left rear, and was connected with it by a gentle undulation.

Seeing that the French really meant business, he gave the order at 1:30 p. m. to strike the camp, and sent for his generals, giving them their instructions verbally to Seydlitz he gave the whole of the cavalry and a free hand, and as soon as the troops were ready to march, they moved off in open column of companies in two lines, left in front, and retired under cover of the above mentioned undulation of the ground. The enemy, seeing this movement, took it to mean a retreat on Merseburg, and continued their march, hoping to reach that place first. Seydlitz, whilst the infantry were preparing to move, rode down and assumed the command of the troops just given him, who were drawn up in two lines behind the infantry, assembled his officers and told them what he intended to do (this was a necessity, as there were no regulations or words of command applicable to larger units than regiments). His intention was to leave some squadrons of hussars to watch the enemy, and with the remainder to move round under cover of the ridge connecting the position on which the camp had been formed with the "Janus Hill," and making this hill a pivot, wheel round and strike the head of the enemy's column.

Having told this to his officers, they rejoined their commands, and he gave the orders: "The left squadron, second line; threes about; remainder left wheel; halt, dress!" and then "March!" The left squadron of the first line swung round on a moving pivot till abreast of the directing squadron of the second line, and the remainder changed direction in succession as they came to the wheeling point, and following on, another change of direction to the right when they reached the above mentioned hill, which had meanwhile been crowned by a battery of eighteen guns (four 24-pounders, twelve 12-pounders, and two howitzers), brought them right across the heads of the three columns in which the French cavalry were advancing. It was just 3:30 p.m. as the last squadron cleared the hill.

Seydlitz, who had been superintending the movement from the hill, seeing he was now almost on the right rear of the enemy, who meanwhile had begun to wheel towards the batteries on the hill, gave the order: "Halt; right wheel into line!" He had fifteen squadrons in first line, and eighteen in second. The hussars, who had been covering his march on the right, cleared the front, and formed up as a support on the left of the line. Then he sounded the trot, and the whole line came over the brow of the hill, to the complete surprise of the French. They tried in vain to wheel up to meet the coming storm, but it was too late, for the next moment the charge was sounded along the whole line, and the Prussians dashed at them at the fullest speed of their horses, swinging round and overlapping the French in rear. The leading regiments bolted and ran, but two Austrian *cuirassier* regiments and two French ones, "*La Reine*" and "*Fitz-James*," managed to get themselves clear of the broken head of the column, and to attempt a charge, but this was met by the following second line of the Prussians, and completely ridden over.

Then followed a sharp pursuit and *mêlée*, in which Seydlitz, having expended all his troops at hand, took part with his sword as an individual. Meanwhile the infantry had appeared on the scene. By a similar flank march under cover, and a wheel into line, they, too, had been thrown across the line of march of the French columns, and their fire and that of the battery, which had advanced from its previous position, prevented all attempts of the French to form line to the front. It was just 4 o'clock as the infantry fire began, and in fifteen minutes the French were shaking. Seydlitz, who had been wounded in the previous *mêlée*, and had fallen out to get himself bandaged, had foreseen what was coming, and had already rallied and re-formed his cavalry, and was waiting for the opportunity, and seized it at once, charging the French on their right flank at full gallop with every available squadron, and by half-past 4 all organised resistance was at an end.

Of the Prussian infantry, seven battalions only had fired a shot, and of these five had fired two rounds per man only, the remaining two from twelve to fifteen rounds each. The Prussians lost 3 officers and 162 men killed, and 20 officers and 356 men wounded, whereas they buried of the dead over 1,000 bodies and picked up some 3,000 wounded, besides capturing 5 generals, 300 officers, 67 guns, 21 standards, any amount of baggage, and 5,000 prisoners, and only the short day put a stop to their pursuit.

It is very difficult to arrive at a fair estimate of the quality of the French troops and their Austrian allies, but they were certainly no riffraff; but, on the contrary, long-service soldiers who had won under the same leaders a fair share of glory—to judge by French accounts, a very large share indeed—in the War of the Spanish Succession. It is not even clear that they were unduly careless, the Prussian Light Cavalry having prevented their seeing what actually was going on. Certainly they must have been considerably superior to the conscripts of the latter years of the Empire, who, nevertheless, as a rule, proved too tough a nut for the Prussian, Austrian, and Russian cavalries to crack during the 1813-14 campaigns. Besides, though the direction of Seydlitz's attack on the infantry was against the flank of the column, yet locally it must have been a frontal one, for the simple order, "Right wheel into line," would bring them into a line far exceeding the front of the Prussian cavalry, and they had ample time to execute this. They were thus even stronger in frontal fire than a line of squares with intervals, but it availed them nothing.

In all military history there is no parallel to this astonishing defeat; for, for all practical purposes, the infantry battalions were not brought into action, and some of the flanking squadrons may be neglected, and we have as a result thirty-eight squadrons, eighteen guns, and seven battalions of, in round numbers, 550 muskets each, defeating in all 64,000 men in one hour from the time the first gun was fired, with an expenditure of infantry ammunition not exceeding (roughly) 16,000 rounds. It is certainly not likely that under any conceivable circumstances such results can be attained by cavalry again; but it is undeniably an absolute and convincing proof of the fallacy of the dogma of the Napoleonic era that "cavalry cannot charge unshaken infantry," for the conditions were identically the same as those under which this dogma was held to be proved.

I have given the words of command for the first charge of the cavalry exactly as they occur in my authority, because the extreme simplicity of the preliminary movements is thereby rendered more apparent; but, simple as they were, Hoenig, In his *Tactical Guides for the Cavalry Division,'* written in 1884, says that it is well known that no cavalry has since succeeded in executing the same movement with equal precision, and no one has yet contradicted him; and he uses this as a proof of the superiority of the individual training of Frederick's cavalry as against that of the present day. What this statement amounts to is that it was impossible in 1884 to find thirty-three squadrons which could be moved by one man about 4,000 yards with two changes of direction at right angles nearly, at a trot, and then wheel into line with sufficient precision.

It is very difficult to catch this author (Hoenig) tripping, but I cannot help thinking that this time he has overlooked the fact that the wheel into line was made "to the halt," and, however the case may have stood in 1884, I think the brigade of ten squadrons that I have seen in Germany during the last two years, galloping in column of troops (*zugs*) for 2,000 yards with a change of direction and subsequent wheel into line on the move could have easily accomplished the above movement even when forming part of a larger body. It would, however, be an interesting problem for our own cavalry to try at our next manoeuvres.

But though the result of the charge was so brilliant, yet Seydlitz's next feat at Zorndorf shows even greater capacity in troops and leader; and it is also of more value, since we can to a certain extent measure the capacity of the Russian infantry for fighting by the fact that they proved themselves fully a match for the Prussian foot soldiers. The battle was fought on the 26th of August, 1758. The Prussians took into action 22,800 infantry in thirty-eight battalions, 9,960 cavalry in eighty-three squadrons, and 117 guns. The Russians numbered some 52,000 men, but were weak in regular cavalry. In their first position they faced at first due east, but as the Prussians kept on continually outflanking them, they at last changed front, right back, till they were jammed in an angle between two boggy streams and could move no further.

Their front was further intersected by two other tributary streams, also in marshy bottoms, which divided their position into a right,

BATTLE OF ZORNDORF

centre, and left wing of about equal strength. It was the intention of the king to attack the Russian right, and for this purpose, he had united sixty guns, twenty battalions, and thirty-six squadrons on his own left, and sent them in, very much as we should do now—namely, the whole of the artillery in two big batteries of twenty and forty guns respectively, covered by an advance guard, and the remainder in two lines ready to attack when the gunners had prepared the way to a certain extent, the separation of the batteries being necessary in this case owing to the conformation of the ground.

The left flank battery appears to have done particularly good work on the Russian position, owing to the density of their formation, four deep lines, one behind the other, and about 200 yards apart, and when the commander of the first Prussian line saw the enemy relieving and supporting his front line by troops out of the second, he ordered his infantry to advance and open fire; but the king's instructions not having been obeyed, the troops in advancing uncovered their outer flank, and the Russians, seizing the opportunity, made a counter-attack with the two front lines of infantry, fairly bore down the Prussians, the Russian regular cavalry charged in on the retreating mob, and in a few minutes fifteen battalions and twenty-six guns were either captured or in full flight. The Russian cavalry did not, however, get out of hand, but halted and formed up, their infantry alone continuing the pursuit.

Meanwhile Seydlitz, with thirty-three squadrons, fifteen of which were *cuirassiers*, the remainder hussars, had been moving round the Russian right on the further side of the boggy valley of the "Zaber," on which their flank rested, and had caused adjutants and pioneers from each regiment to reconnoitre and improve passages across it broad enough for half troop front. Seeing what was happening on the other side of the stream, he now ordered each regiment to advance in column of half troops from its right and cross the stream by the above mentioned passages, two regiments (ten squadrons) of *cuirassiers* to attack the pursuing infantry, and the remaining regiment, his own, to charge the enemy's cavalry, the hussars to follow as a second line. These orders were obeyed.

As each regiment crossed the bottom, it formed line to the front at the gallop, and went straight for its target. The shock of the first line was not everywhere successful, but the prompt support of the following hussars completed the work; and after a few minutes of hand-to-hand combat, the Russian cavalry was drawn from the field and their advanced infantry practically destroyed. They were pursued up to the line of their own position in rear, which in the meanwhile had been completed by great reserves, and there the rally was sounded, and Seydlitz withdrew out of range of the musketry and re-formed his command, which had meanwhile been reinforced by the remaining squadrons of the right wing, which had stood originally behind the infantry, which had been defeated and had come back on them in complete rout; but, wheeling up their squadrons to let the fugitives through, they had again wheeled into line and charged the pursuing foe in their front at the gallop at the same moment that Seydlitz's *cuirassiers* and hussars attacked them in the flank.

The Russians, however, had defended themselves with unusual desperation; trained in the Turkish wars neither to ask nor expect quarter, they had balled themselves into clumps, and the cavalry had had to hew them to pieces.

But Seydlitz, having rallied his squadrons, now determined to attack the remainder of the Russian right, which still stood in battle order before him. Though they had brought up fresh reserves, the retreat of their cavalry had left their outer flank exposed, and, he decided to avail himself of the opportunity. Taking with him three *cuirassier* regiments, which stood in three lines at about 150 yards' distance, he wheeled them into column of squadrons, left in front, and trotted right past the Russian right, and then wheeled them into line to the right and delivered his charge. The Russians were trying to close up the gaps between their lines by wheeling back the outer companies, but they were caught in the act, and the whole mass, all who stood on the plateau between the two streams, and who formed the right wing of the army, were ridden down and exterminated.

The Russian centre lay thus uncovered, its right resting on a similar marshy hollow to that across which the first attack had been made; but for the moment the risk of a third charge with his blown and disordered squadrons seemed to Seydlitz too great to be undertaken. He therefore withdrew them behind Zorndorf, at a walk, in open column of squadrons. Meanwhile, the king had set his centre's right in motion, the centre refused, and the artillery was sent on in front to prepare the attack at case-shot range. In executing this movement the guns on the right advanced too far, and were immediately assailed by a swarm of Cossacks, who captured the pieces, rode down their immediate escort, and then boldly attacked the following battalions; but these, notwithstanding the confusion caused by the bolting teams with the limbers, reserved their fire till the enemy were within 50 paces, and then delivered a steady volley, and before they had recovered from its effect twenty-two squadrons of Prussian cavalry charged them, defeated them, and retook the guns.

The Prussian infantry continued their advance, and had just opened fire when the Russian regular cavalry rode at them, and no less than thirteen battalions, seized by panic, in terror broke and fled. For the moment it seemed that victory must remain with the Russians. It was again Seydlitz who turned the scale; he had meanwhile collected and re-formed the sixty-one squadrons—over 7,000 sabres—and had formed them in three lines, eighteen squadrons of *cuirassiers* in the first, fifteen of dragoons in the second, and twenty-eight of hussars in the third, at 250 paces' distance, one behind the other. The horses were much done up, having been twelve hours under their riders, to say nothing of their previous charges.

He had been following the movement of the infantry in echelon on their left flank, and on seeing their flight he sounded the "gallop," and then "shouldered" them round till they overlapped the Russian right. Knowing that the Russians were in the habit of throwing themselves down to let the cavalry pass over them and then rising to pour a fire into their backs, he had determined to charge with one line covering the other, and to lead the first line himself. Owing to the fatigue of the horses, the pace was at first little more than a canter. For a moment all firing ceased and nothing was heard but the ever-growing thunder of the horses' hoofs.

The Russians had quickly closed the gaps between their lines and brought up every available gun, 100 in all, to bear on the advancing mass, and almost simultaneously the whole opened fire with case, tearing wide gaps in the opposing ranks. Fortunately for the Prussians, their outer flank, to avoid the marshy ground beyond them, had been crowding on the centre, and this crowding, usually so dangerous, was here advantageous, as it caused the gaps to close quicker, and the charge was thus delivered almost in a wall and swept right over the infantry, notwithstanding their fire, delivered at the shortest range, from twelve successive ranks. There was no panic in the Russian ranks; the men stood their ground to the last, and no quarter was given or asked, and the rest of the day was simply a combat of man against man, till sheer weariness put a stop to the fighting, and the intact troops of the Russian left managed to effect a retreat because no fresh forces were at hand to receive them.

Altogether the Russian loss on this day, killed, wounded, and missing, amounted to 21,550 officers and men, 103 guns, and 27 stand of colours, or 40 *per cent*, approximately, of their strength; the Prussians, 11,380 out of 30,000, the bulk of which fell on the infantry; and our own losses at Inkermann are the only ones I know to compare to the above—*i. e.*, as borne by the victors, but our numbers on that occasion were too small to make the comparison fair, as a whole.

But to appreciate Seydlitz's exploit fairly, and to judge from his example what may reasonably be expected from first-rate cavalry, one or two points deserve to be specially noticed. Infantry tends to improve under the conditions of war as then waged by the Russians—namely, sufficient fighting and not too much marching—and these infantry had further been trained in war against the Turks to stand shoulder to shoulder and fight to the last, as quarter was never given on either side. This method of war brought out the very best qualities of the Russian soldier—the power of stubborn resistance.

The Prussian cavalry, on the other hand, was far from having reached its zenith, for they had suffered much from the previous campaigns, and, owing to these and the large augmentations the war entailed, its ranks were filled with a disproportionate number of recruits, whose training as horsemen had had to be conducted under the difficulties of dispersal in small bodies over large areas during winter quarters; and this final and greatest charge was made under conditions which subsequently the French laid down as impossible—namely, after being rallied from two previous charges. It will be remembered that it was an axiom in the French school, and one largely adopted subsequently in our own, that cavalry once sent in to the attack could not be again relied on for action a second time during the day; yet this was their third charge. That such a feat was possible can only be explained by the excellent system of individual training in the control of the horse, which had become traditional in the army from previous campaigns and which was rapidly taught to the recruits by the example and precept of the older veterans with whom they served.

The true culminating point of cavalry efficiency was only reached some years after the conclusion of the Seven Years' War, when the country had had time to recover from its terrible losses and the ranks were again filled with horses in the prime of their strength and men who had been adequately trained to ride them. By that time, too, some ten years after the Hubertsburg peace, Seydlitz had not only perfected his system, but had trained an adequate number of subordinates to understand it, and all ranks had been quickened by actual experience, and taught only that which was useful in the field. Unfortunately, the details of the system as practiced have to a great extent been forgotten. The best general account of them will be found in Prince Hohenlohe's *Gespräche über Kavallerie*, above alluded to, a book which would, if translated, prove even of greater value to the British cavalry than the well-known instructions of General von Schmidt; but incomplete as the evidence admittedly is, it has been sufficient to completely transform the German cavalry, which in capacity for manoeuvres, endurance of its horses, and in a general confidence in its own power pervading all ranks, is now, perhaps, four times as efficient as in 1870.

Of course, the relation between cavalry and infantry can never be absolute, but will vary on every battlefield, and, indeed, with every hour; but because at the conclusion of a long campaign, when the material on which much of its success depends—its horses—have sunk to the lowest ebb, it fails, as at Waterloo, to ride down first-rate infantry. Training it in peacetime to distrust its own power is the greatest error that possibly can be made; and if in 1866 and 1870 cavalry failed to effect all that might justly have been expected of them, the armies which chose to adopt such views cannot blame the cavalry. Had the Germans at Vionville possessed the spirit and leaders they now can claim, the Sixth Cavalry Division would not have arrived too late. Bredow's charge, if necessary at all, would have been made with at least thirty squadrons instead of six, and the final charge of the day on the plateau north of Mars-la-Tour by some seventy-two squadrons, with results proportionately greater than they actually were.

The Germans are still behind the ideal of Seydlitz's day. Whether they can ever attain to it with three years' service in the ranks is open to doubt. Of all nations in the world, it seems to me that we are the only one that has both time and material for the task. Undoubtedly we have serious difficulties to contend with, chief among which is the dispersion of our squadrons in small garrisons—this, however, is no worse than the winter quarters in which Seydlitz's recruits were trained; and next to this comes the necessity of putting young horses half trained in the ranks. Both of these are primarily a matter of money, and the second would in a very short time prove a source of economy, for, for each month's additional training under six years of age we should get two of useful work at the other end of their service.

But the principal change, on which the ultimate efficiency of the whole depends and without which no conceivable reform can succeed, would not cost the country a farthing, and could be initiated by an order from the commander-in-chief tomorrow. It is simply the adoption of the squadron system—*i. e.,* every squadron leader to be responsible for the drill efficiency of his squadron, and for the colonel to command four squadrons, and not, as at present, 500 men and horses, more or less. For, unless each captain can be relied on to have his squadron exactly in the position required, all movement of larger bodies become impossible; but to do this he must not only have experience in leading it as a whole, but must also have the incentive which only personal responsibility can give to take the trouble to learn.

This was the weak point in our organisation, which last year's Berkshire cavalry manoeuvres disclosed, but to which as yet no one has called attention. Yet this alone can remedy the defects therein disclosed. Not even a Seydlitz could have done anything with the squadrons there assembled, for, to begin with, 30 *per cent* would have been down with sore backs before they met the enemy. Now, "sore backs" are a consequence of defective stable management, and defective stable management again results from over-centralization of control.

With few exceptions, our present regimental system amounts to this: All executive power is centred in the orderly-room, and the squadron officers are robbed of all incentive to exertion. The consequence is that they meet the spirit of things half way, and take as much leave as they can get. This is very much pleasanter than hanging about barracks with little or nothing to do. Meanwhile the adjutant drills the regiment, and now and again the colonel takes it, and then, and only then, the squadron officers take their places in front of their commands. Then the trouble begins, for however well the adjutant may have prepared the regiment, his own personal power of command cannot be handed over to another man, nor can the squadrons follow their officers as they may have learnt to follow their substitutes on adjutant's parades. Thus the colonel is deprived of the aid of the very men who alone render his task possible.

This is meant for an extreme case, and one that is daily becoming less common, but the difference is one of degree, not of principle. The system of squadron training is an immense advance, but it is to be feared that its true scope is as yet hardly grasped. Its object should be to give squadron commanders a chance of learning how to lead their squadrons, and to acquire over them that personal influence which is as necessary to efficiency in a squadron as it is to a bandmaster over his band. It is an undefinable personal relation between leader and led, and cannot be arbitrarily transferred from one to another. And, actually, it is the only thing which really signifies, for reconnaissance duties, outposts, and all the other details usually taught in the training, could be equally well, and even better, taught by a single expert for the whole regiment.

It is usually urged as an objection to the German system that our officers would not consent to work as hard as our comrades on the other side of the channel. Personally, I doubt this. Given the same incentive, an Englishman's spirit of emulation is as keen as that of any other nationality. But if the work were organised on proper lines, it need not be harder, if as hard, as it is at present. Let the recruits and remounts still be trained by the adjutant and riding master. They are specially picked men, and will probably do it better than any others. Let the adjutant, with one or two other selected officers, further take over the instruction in all subjects which do not call for the precise movements of closed squadrons, and then let the squadron commanders devote themselves exclusively for the time of training to acquiring a real personal control and power of handling their men. When they are perfect in that, the colonel can take over the regiment and lead his four squadrons without any anxiety, for everyone will be in his right place and know his work.

Few of our critics appear to recognize the really admirable keenness and soldierly spirit which exists in many of our cavalry regiments. The officers are as keen as those that exist in any service. One fault is that we allow that keenness to be directed into side channels instead of concentrating it on the one main issue. If men were once encouraged and given the opportunity to learn what leadership really means, their anxiety to retain and increase it would soon lead them to perfect themselves in the minor details of their work. Equitation, as well as cross-country riding, would be studied, and we would soon have a cavalry even more perfect in the control of their horses than our present model, the German. For, after all, we do possess the best material and double the time to work it into shape.

General Marbot's Memoirs

The three substantial volumes which contain the life and experiences of General Baron Marbot,[1] one of the soldiers of the French Revolution and Empire, may perhaps frighten would-be readers by their bulk, as they did me for a time; but those who will venture to tackle them will, I think, find themselves richly rewarded.

Indeed, in the 1200 odd pages there is hardly one that will bear skipping; the book is simply absorbingly interesting from cover to cover, yet it is a work in which one has constantly to apply corrections for personal error. Marbot Was evidently personally exceedingly plucky, and by temperament always looked on the bright side of things. This latter was by no means the tendency of many other French Writers who have contributed to the history of the last campaigns, notably the Russian retreat of 1812; and, generally speaking, the worst pessimists have obtained the most readers, simply because the average individual likes his dish of horrors hot and strong.

Ségur,[2] whose account of the retreat is about the best known, next to that of Thiers, and who had the advantage of an almost inimitable gift of style, has done very much to perpetuate the legend of the exceptional horrors of that event, and yet there is a vast amount of evidence on the other side, which is and has been available for years, which should have made military history students shy of him ages ago.

Since it is utterly impossible to refer to one-tenth of the events

---

1. Republished by Leonaur - *The Young Hussar: French Cavalryman of the Napoleonic Wars at Marengo, Austerlitz, Jena, Eylau and Friedland* v. 1, *The Imperial Aide-de-camp: French Cavalryman of the Napoleonic Wars at Saragossa, Landshut, Eckmuhl, Ratisbon, Aspern-Essling, Wagram, Busaco and Torres Vedras* v. 2 and *The Colonel of Chasseurs: French Cavalryman of the Napoleonic Wars in the Retreat from Moscow, Lutzen, Bautzen, Katzbach, Leipzig, Hanau and Waterloo* v. 3.
2. *Aide-de-Camp to Napoleon* by Philippe-Paul de Ségur also published by Leonaur.

which Marbot so graphically describes within the limits of either my time or space, and since, moreover. General Sir George Chesney has already dealt with the earlier portions of this work, I purpose to fix my attention principally on this one point and the campaign of the succeeding year.

It so happens that only a few years ago, and before I had reached the period in Marbot's work, I was talking to a retired Prussian general, well known in the historical section of the General Staff here, on this very point, and he told me that not only from the archives which he has consulted, but from his personal knowledge of many of the Prussian families whose grandfathers went with Napoleon to Moscow, and who returned alive, he is convinced that the actual losses of the Grand Army have been enormously overrated; that the army broke up and melted away is beyond dispute, but that they all died there is another matter altogether.

I remember re-reading Ségur up at Quetta during some specially bitter weather and talking over subsequently at mess the hardships and degree of cold endured by our troops in the last Afghan war. I checked the statements as near as I could from official returns, and compared them with Ségur's observations. I have not the notes at hand to refer to, but my recollection is that we stood actually more cold in Afghanistan that the French did in Russia, and that many of our men were by no means better clad than the French, rather the reverse.

If one takes Marbot's account of the passage of the Beresina, or, indeed, any other one, it is perfectly apparent that the cold then was by no means intense, for the stream, which could not have had more than one mile an hour velocity of current, and not over 40 feet in width, was not frozen over, but only covered with drift ice. What is more, it was nowhere more than 4 feet deep, and it does not require much experience to know that a stream of this nature will freeze without any very intense frost at all. I have again and again seen the Ouse at York, with a 2-knot current, 200 feed; in width, and 20 feet deep, frozen and with people skating on it, and everyone can recall cases of the Thames frozen over about Windsor within their own lifetime.

But all order and discipline had ceased in the French Army, except in a few picked corps, long before their arrival at the Beresina on the 28th of November. Marbot and his regiment, the 23rd Chasseurs (cavalry), had been with St. Cyr at Pultosk, and only rejoined the Moscow army at, but on the wrong side of, the river, and from his account it is perfectly evident that practically everyone, staff and all, were numbed with cold and gave no orders whatever. Thus, after the bridges were finished on the first day (and, it being a moonlight night, there was nothing whatever to prevent their being made use of to evacuate the trains and stragglers), the two bridges lay open and unutilized for the whole of the night, say fourteen hours, and in that time at least 60,000 men or their equivalents in trains, etc., might easily have passed. As a fact, too, the stream was almost everywhere fordable to wagons and horses, and when the great crush came next day, hundreds did ford it only to perish at the opposite bank, because it had not occurred to anyone to ramp it down, though men, tools, and time were all available.

Neither were the men starving from either hunger or cold at the time. There was fuel enough and to spare to cook all the dead horses in the place, and of these there seems to have been an ample supply. Horseflesh is perhaps not quite an epicure's ideal when toasted over a wood fire, but I take it that hungry men accustomed to bear hardship would not refuse it anyway.

The Beresina is always taken to have been the culminating crisis of the retreat. After that, the cold became more intense certainly, but the greater majority of the men who survived that event managed somehow or other to reach the frontier. Marbot, who never seems to have been wanting in expedients, made sledges for his men, and hitched the horses on to them, and appears to have got along comfortably enough, though he himself was suffering from a terrible lance wound, which had penetrated his knee-cap and passed between the joint of the thighbone and lower part of the leg.

It is worth while here pointing out that his own regiment crossed the Niemen at the beginning of the campaign 1,018 strong, received 30 recruits, and ultimately recrossed the same river with 663; of the rest, 109 were killed in action, 65 wounded, 77 prisoners, and 104 missing. Certainly he had not been to Moscow, but he had been more frequently under fire than the others, and came in for the worst part of the retreat; but his careful forethought for the men was what really reduced his losses.

His estimate of the total loss of the Grand Army, based on a return he claims to have seen in the hands of Gourgaud, and covered with notes in Napoleon's own writing, is arrived at as follows: Grand total of all nations that passed the Niemen, 325,000; of these, 155,400 French, and 176,500 allies; these latter disbanded of their own account immediately on regaining their frontiers, and their losses cannot be accurately stated, but 60,000 French re-crossed the river, leaving a balance over of 95,000, of whom 30,000 were taken prisoners and ultimately reached their native country after the peace of 1814, so that 65,000 only actually died in Russia, and half of these, at least, must have been killed in action.

Another point which shows that the actual state of depression cannot have been so great as is usually imagined is, that in spite of all the hardships the black-guard element in the army kept up its spirits remarkably well, and even found energy enough to dress up at night as Cossacks, alarm the bivouacs, and steal, murder, and plunder all they could lay hands on. Most of these men, he tells us, were Poles, and a whole gang was caught by an ambuscade laid by some of the men who preserved a certain amount of discipline. They were brought before General Maison, and stated in defence that they only did it for a joke, but Maison said this was not the time or place for joking, and had the whole gang shot on the spot, after which no more was heard of these ruffians. Now in time of real hardship this class of black-guard usually goes to the wall first, not last; things cannot have been so bad if they retained pluck enough for such combined atrocities.

In fact, the more one looks into this campaign, the more convinced does one become that want of discipline was the primary cause of the whole disaster; and again, that want of discipline is directly traceable to the system of centralization Napoleon had himself introduced. He had cowed Berthier and most of his marshals. Marbot gives many instances in which the former, both in this and the subsequent campaigns, when called on for instructions by corps and divisional commanders, pimply replied, "*Pas d'ordres*," and took no trouble to get any. In consequence, the supply service which Napoleon believed to exist was not attended to at all except in the Guards with whom he marched, and from the very first days of the campaign the men had to struggle to find food, and thus by degrees all semblance of discipline was lost.

How this state of affairs originated, and when, is best seen in the pages of Fezensac,[3] who, I take it, was a more accurate if less optimistic observer than Marbot. Fezensac, of whose work an admirable summary is given by the late Colonel Chesney in his military biographies, shows that this relaxation of all discipline began in the early days of the Grand Army in the march to Ulm, and though not directly corroborated by Marbot, though he is by many other writers, indirectly

3. *A Journal of the Russian Campaign of 1812* by Raymond A. P. J. de Montesquiou-Fezensac also published by Leonaur.

much confirmation is to be had out of the latter's (Marbot's) pages.

Now the above sheds a good deal of light on the otherwise almost inexplicable resurrection of the French fighting strength in the following years. It is certain that those who did return from Russia were undeniably the survivors of the fittest. Only the bravest, best disciplined, and constitutionally strongest pulled through, and 60,000 of these were enough to leaven any array. Then Marbot gives some information as to the nature of the fresh troops forwarded from the *dépôts*; a large number of these were undeniably exceedingly unwilling troops of the nature with which Erckmann-Chatrian's[4] works have made us familiar, others belonged to the recalcitrant class, details of which I have dwelt upon in a previous article, but Marbot tells us there were also 40,000 men of the so-called *compagnies departmentales*, the Guards of the *prefete*, who had selected the best and smartest men for their own personal glorification, and these had for the most part been well quartered and carefully drilled for a term of years, and only wanted the "baptism of fire" to become first-rate troops, and with the survivors of Russia were enough to leaven more than double their number of less well trained and disposed conscripts.

Add to this the confidence of all in Napoleon[5] himself, and the executive ability of his marshals and divisional leaders when under his immediate eyes, and the extraordinary successes he *himself* managed to achieve become in part explicable. I say he *himself*, because his marshals in this campaign, acting alone, almost invariably succeeded in getting thoroughly beaten.

Perhaps the most invaluable parts of his work are the side-lights he throws on the personal characteristics of these marshals,[6] and, as *aide-de-camp* to Augereau, Lannes, and Masséna, few men can speak with greater authority.

Lannes was his favourite, and from the portrait he gives of him it is easy to understand why. Lannes was brave, straightforward, and generous, and particularly thoughtful for all around him. He nursed Marbot after his terrible injuries at Eylau, when the latter had been picked up stark-naked all but one boot from the snow-clad frozen ground, and he himself ultimately died in Marbot's arms.

Chesney has already given the incidents of Marbot's disasters that

---

4. *The Napoleonic Novels:*Volumes 1 and 2 by Erckmann-Chatrian also published by Leonaur.

5. *Napoleon's Campaign in Russia 1812* by Achilles Rose also published by Leonaur.

6. *Napoleon's Marshals* by R. P. Dunn-Pattison also published by Leonaur.

day at Eylau, but they will bear repetition. The celebrated "*14th de Ligne*" had been ordered to hold a little hillock in the plain, and were doing so against overwhelming odds. They were practically surrounded by clouds of Cossacks and other troops, and the order to retire had to be sent to them. One after another, two gallopers started and never arrived; it was Marbot's turn next. Lannes, who loved the boy (for he was little more than that in age) like his own son, gave him the message with tears in his eyes, and Marbot was riding a perfect man-eating devil of a horse, which, as a rule, was only quiet on the battlefield, and which he had only tamed by the original dodge of taking with him to the stable a red-hot leg of roast mutton; when the horse, which had just eaten a groom, made a rush at him, Marbot shoved the steaming joint in its mouth. The animal seized it and worried it, and the more it worried the worse it got burnt.

As a consequence, it came to the conclusion that its master was a bad character to tackle, and towards him (and another groom, who tried the same trick) it became perfectly docile. Now, watching his brother officers. Marbot had noticed that they had all ridden with drawn swords, and endeavoured to defend themselves. Knowing the speed and devilment of his animal, he returned his sword, took up the reins in both hands, and set her (it was a mare) going, and by sheer speed reached the hill untouched. But there was then no means of executing the order, and as he was stopping to speak to the colonel, a round shot grazed the back of his head-gear and utterly paralyzed his limbs by the shock. He saw everything going on around him, but was powerless to move a limb. For some minutes he sat there, his horse as quiet as a lamb, whilst the 14th fell as they stood in their ranks.

They were ultimately entirely destroyed, till suddenly a Russian, who had succeeded in coming within reach, aimed a vicious thrust at him, but missed and struck the mare, and the smart of the wound woke up the sleeping devil within her. Springing forward, she seized the wretched man by the jaw, tore the lower part of his face clean away, and then dashed right out through the enemy and galloped back towards the French lines. For a time Marbot kept his seat (he was riding in an old Hungarian saddle, and, as he says, he could not fall out of it), but at length loss of blood—he had received two additional wounds—caused him to faint, and he fell on the snow, where he lay for hours insensible.

A French trooper coming by took him for dead, and, attracted by his brilliant new uniform—he (Marbot) was fresh from Paris—

stopped to strip him, and did so all but his last boot, which he could not get off, as one of the wounds had caused the foot to swell. The pain brought Marbot round, and, seeing signs of life, the plunderer bolted.

Meanwhile the mare had got safely back and been found by his servant, a most devoted man to his master's interests. Fearing the worst, this servant went back to the battlefield; it was then dark, but by a bivouac fire he found the man who had plundered his master, and recognized the new uniform at once, and asked the man where he had got it from. It was the custom of war to plunder the dead in that army, and the fellow was not at all a robber, but at once offered to go back and show the place, and so it happened that just as the intense cold was beginning to have its effect, the rescuing party turned up and Marbot was saved.

Augereau's life would require a volume to itself. He had been a private in the Prussian Army, but had deserted, and, after a most adventurous career, reached France just at the right moment, and rapidly rose to the command of a corps and the marshal's baton. It happened curiously enough that during the campaign of Jena his corps took the whole of his old regiment prisoners, and Augereau found his old senior lieutenant commanding his old company, and most of the sergeants still in the same old grades. Their astonishment when they were brought before their conqueror, former private of Prussia, now marshal of France, must have been as great as, if not greater than, that of Joseph's brethren in Egypt.

Augereau, however, behaved better than Joseph, and did not accuse them of petty larceny, but did as well as he could—gave them all a most liberal tip, and saw to it that they were as well treated as circumstances would permit. The portions of the book that deal with the Spanish campaigns are of quite exceptional interest to English readers, though he accuses us (or rather, some of our officers) of acts of bad military faith, breach of parole, and so forth. Our successes he ascribes, amongst other causes, to two in particular: the excellence of our *shooting* and the perfection of our scouting carried out by our officers, who, mounted on thoroughbreds, rode close up to their columns and counted every man and gun with impunity, for their cavalry could never catch them, for at the first obstacle, which our men trained in the hunting-field negotiated without difficulty, the French fell off and had to pick themselves up again. It seems, therefore, that we have not really so much to learn from the German scouting in the Sedan march as people usually suppose.

One cause, however, of our successes, which so far, I believe, has never been referred to, was of a social nature, and there was at woman at the bottom of it, as usual.

Most of the senior officers in Spain, notably Junot, had their wives with them, but the" lady who accompanied Masséna had omitted the ceremony of going to church with him. The other ladies declined to meet her, and hence arose endless quarrels between the generals. Again, since Masséna could not leave her behind, the march of the columns had to be timed, not to suit exactly her convenience, but the limit of her physical endurance, for she was a brave woman and never made difficulties if she could help it, and Marbot speaks highly of the pluck and courage she showed. Still it rather discounts one's pride in the exploits of our men to find that to a certain extent these were only possible because of a woman weakness on the opposite side. But reverse the picture, and imagine one of our leaders in a similar plight.

Attack of Defence

As my readers are aware, I have never been much of a believer in the virtues of the defensive in war, but in the course of some studies I have recently been making as to the effect of improvements in armament, smokeless powder, etc., on the problem stated above, I have found that the case against the defence is even worse than I had supposed, and have arrived at a method of stating the problem much clearer than any I have as yet submitted.

Broadly the question may be stated thus: Assuming equality of armament, training, and mobility in the contending armies, as the number of the troops engaged increases, a limit is reached beyond which victory for the defender becomes inconceivable, and for this reason: as the length of the line held by the defence increases, the uncertainty at which point in this line the chief blow will fall becomes ever greater. To meet this, either the line must be made equally strong at all points, which would require a great numerical superiority, or the reserves must be held back in some central position at a considerable distance from the front line.

Again, the larger the reserves the slower their rate of movement, and this statement holds good even when marching on a broad front across country; a whole corps cannot get over the ground as rapidly as a single battalion. Hence the larger the army the longer it will take to support any given point in the line.

Now, the time within which the arrival of the reserve can turn threatened defeat into victory is limited by the time which the weapons in use require in order to prepare the way for a successful attack; and the greater the power of the weapons the more rapid their effect; and the greater the total number available the more there will be to put in at the decisive attack, for fewer will be required to carry out a purely delaying action on other parts of the line. But the rapidity with which the work of preparation can be accomplished increases in a much higher ratio than the number of guns engaged.

Modern improvements, particularly in artillery, have all tended to increase the number of guns that can be usefully employed on a given front. The greatly extended range and the gain in accuracy of fire not only allows a far wider latitude in choice of position, but enables two, and even three, tiers of guns to be in simultaneous action against the same target, an advantage of which the Germans frequently availed themselves in the last manoeuvres. Again, the absence of smoke renders, it possible to place guns at closer intervals without interfering with each other's fire, and the attack can make use of indirect fire, from behind cover, to an extent not possible to the defender, who must have his guns sufficiently far advanced to protect their own front against assault on pain of incurring worse troubles if he fails to do so.

The first indication the defender can receive of the point on which the blow is intended to fall will be the sudden deployment of an overwhelming artillery mass, and even then the inference cannot be jumped at, for there is nothing to prevent the sudden withdrawal of guns in action at a long range, and their transference in a body to some other point six or seven miles away, provided always that they have been trained to manoeuvre collectively.

Supposing, for instance, an army of four corps attacking with three in first line, one in reserve, over ground not absolutely uniform in slope. The three corps open the fight from every available gun along the whole front. Those of the right-hand corps have orders to endeavour to get in to within 2,500 yards before unlimbering; the others, not to commit themselves so deeply.

The artillery of the corps in reserve comes up and deploys some 1,000 yards to the rear of the guns on the right, half of them perhaps out of sight behind a wave of the ground.

The mere fact that the first deployment on the right indicated an intention to get in closer will have attracted the enemy's attention to that flank, and the appearance of reinforcements will tend to confirm it. Orders are sent off to move up the reserves. Then the assailant withdraws the artillery of his reserve corps—the guns under cover moving first, of course—and transfers the whole mass of them along the rear of the troops in action from right to left, where they dash in through the intervals of the batteries already on the ground, and unlimber at once, perhaps at 1,500 yards. That such a movement could not be attempted with badly trained or indifferently handled troops is, of course, admitted, but a capable staff ought surely to be able to reconnoitre and clear the way for such a manoeuvre, and the distance, say 6 to 7 miles, is not an insuperable obstacle, but brigade drill and the habit of manoeuvring at a gallop would alone guarantee its success.

The immediate result on the other side would be confusion and counter-orders, in itself, no small gain to the assailants, and whilst things were being readjusted a very unequal struggle would be taking place. Unfortunately, we have no practical data on which to decide the question, How long would it take 250 guns to silence 125 at a mean range of 2,500 yards? Prince Hohenlohe tells us of Prussian gunners who maintain that half an hour ought to be sufficient to settle the matter one way or the other, even as between equal numbers; but, as he proceeds to point out, this is probably immensely overestimated; but against a two-fold superiority an hour ought certainly to suffice, for the moment one side obtains the upper hand the process of destruction goes on with cumulative forces. Then, once the defenders' guns had been forced to retire, either to refit or really knocked out of action, the assailant can move his artillery up to thoroughly effective range, if they are not already there, and then the duel between the French infantry and the German artillery on the Rotherberg at Spicheren gives us some data to go upon.

In that case eight Prussian guns were unlimbered under circumstances of extreme difficulty, successively and not simultaneously, against eight companies of steady long-service French infantry behind a substantial entrenchment at 800 yards' range, and after half an hour's fighting, during which the gunners suffered very heavy loss, being entirely unprotected, the infantry were compelled to evacuate their trenches and to retire.

Any modern gun is as effective at 1,800 yards today as the old Krupps were at 800 in 1870, even with ordinary common shell, and with the new high explosives considerably more so; whereas no modern rifle is nearly as good at 1,800 yards as the old Chassepôt at 800. And as for fire-discipline, though it is more taught now than then, it is open to question whether any short-service troops of today, (as at time of first publication), will prove steadier under fire than the old long-service soldiers of France, largely seasoned as they were with war-experienced veterans case-hardened to the horrors of a battlefield.

An hour and a half would, therefore, be about all the defenders could count on to move up their reserve, and half the time would probably have been lost had the ruse described above been successful, so that the assailant has a very fair chance of beating his opponent in detail before their arrival.

However, we will not contest this particular point, for it seems to me that even without this advantage, the attack would still have largely the better chance.

Assume for the defence the most favourable type of position possible, a long course, slope of ground dipping gently for 500 yards from the crest, on which the artillery are posted, and then falling more steeply to a water-course or drainage channel some 500 yards further below, so that a line of infantry posted just below where the two slopes intersect have a clear field of fire to their immediate front, and can sweep the opposite sides of the valley over which the enemy has to pass to attack. Such positions are not frequent, but if one thinks the matter out, it will be found that it is the most favourable type conceivable for defence, and any deviation from it only increases the difficulty for the defender. A convex slope facilitates the ranging of the attacking guns, and enables them to keep up their fire longer over the heads of the advancing infantry.

A uniform slope compels the defender to place his first line yet further in advance of his guns, and enables the first line to watch their destruction, and also uniform slopes of this extent are rarely met with in nature; and a perfectly horizontal plain would be worse still, for it would compel guns and infantry to stand in the same line, to each other's mutual inconvenience. Further, though practically a convex slope perfectly uniform in section for many miles nowhere exists in nature, yet it will be found that the nearer it approaches this type the more favourable it will be for the defender, for lateral hollows and drainage lines only increase the difficulty of direct defence, and afford opportunities to the enemy of covered approach.

The question of longer slopes comes under a somewhat different category, for, as a rule, these tend to mask the artillery on both sides, and then the fight is decided by infantry alone; and equally we may leave out of account very steep or precipitous ones, for these favour only the passive defence, and hinder the defenders' ultimate counter-attack, whilst, if he elects the passive defence alone, they can be masked by a few troops in the front, and the remainder marched around against his flanks with perfect impunity.

A course slope as described above is the most favourable for the defence, and now mark what happens. A line of guns committed to the passive defence of a position cannot be left unprotected by infantry in front, for, under cover of even the slightest convexity or unevenness of the ground, light infantry can skirmish up to them and pick off the gunners, who are tied by their position, and cannot manoeuvre backward to get out of the way. Hence infantry must be pushed well out to the front to protect them, and to such a distance that they themselves have a clear field of fire; therefore, to beyond the break in the slope. As I have often pointed out before in dealing with this subject, the supports to this line cannot be placed between it and the guns, partly because of the danger to them from shells bursting prematurely (a danger which may be ignored in the last few minutes of an assault, but not when it may last for a considerable time), partly because they would form too favourable targets being out on the exposed slope for the enemy's artillery; and they cannot be placed immediately behind the guns, for then they would act as stop-butts for all the "overs" meant for the artillery.

When, therefore, the gunners are forced to retire, the first line of infantry will find itself in an exceedingly isolated position, nearer to the enemy, probably, than they are to their own supports.

Now, in any case, a decisive battle is not fought out by a single line, but consists of a gradual bleeding to death of the two opposing forces. Fresh troops are fed up to the rear on either side, and the side which has to feed them up the faster is sooner exhausted; when the way stands open to the enemy's reserves.

The defender has to bring his reinforcements forward down a long slope in the full sweep of the assailants' shrapnel and infantry fire. Judging by what Prince Hohenlohe tells us of the efforts of the French to advance against his guns from Amanvillers, and by what friends of mine present through all the Metz battles have frequently told me, I hardly believe that any troops in Europe exist which could be trusted to face such an ordeal. But we will assume them to be of ideal courage and ultimately to reach their fighting line. Still it must be evident that they will bring a much smaller reinforcement, both in numbers and morale, with them than the supports of the attacking lines advancing only under infantry fire.

Hence, even if we assume a numerical equality between the two infantries, the defender must be bled to death first at this spot, when, of course, if the balance on the side of the assailant is only a couple of battalions, the victory must remain in his hands. I had several opportunities of watching a defender attempting to meet this difficulty in the recent French manoeuvres, but I never saw it satisfactorily solved, and can see no way out of it myself.

For a long time it seemed to me that, given a sufficiently powerful cavalry to protect the artillery against the enemy's horse, the defender might trust to the guns to protect their own front, assisted merely by a few light infantry skirmishers, and place his infantry some 600 to 800 yards in rear of them. Then, when forced to retire, pass through the intervals of the infantry and come into action again a mile or so to the rear. The attacking artillery could not hope to unlimber within 600 yards or so of hitherto unshaken troops, and the infantry, following on behind, would be thrown on their own resources; but even here their supports would be fed up unseen, and they must, therefore, soon establish their fire superiority over the defender, whose movements would be visible.

The final assault downhill would be the difficulty, for then they would have to face the enemy's artillery fire in the open; but, from the nature of the case, this arm must have already suffered very severely in the preliminary duel, and once the infantry fire superiority had been acquired by the assailant, there would be no longer the fire of unshaken infantry to prevent a sufficient number of guns being brought up to keep those of the enemy in check. This, too, would afford a capital opportunity of breaking through the defenders' infantry by a mass charge of cavalry brought up under cover of the hill on which the defenders' artillery originally stood. But even this plan has many disadvantages, more particularly the opening of an action with a retrograde movement, and it could scarcely be put into execution by a large force.

In fact, the more the matter is investigated the more certain does it become that nothing is to be hoped for from the "defensive," except when dealing with very small bodies, or under exceptional circumstances of ground. A force possessing as marked a superiority in discipline and steadiness over the remaining forces of Europe as our old Peninsular Army had over the French might possibly attempt the game with success, though again only in small bodies; but to hear people talk as they do here in England of taking up a position and defending it with our rabble of militia and Volunteers, supported by a totally inadequate proportion of inefficient field guns, makes one's very soul sick. Fortunately, as long as our present naval policy is adhered to, the danger is not very imminent; but who can tell how long it will last, once the other party gets into power?

It is frequently asserted and believed that our close country gives the half-trained troops on the defensive an advantage. This is an utter delusion. Every species of cover which allows of the unobserved approach of the enemy is a disadvantage to the defence under all circumstances, and every copse or hedgerow which interferes with the mobility of troops tells against them in a rapidly increasing ratio to their want of training. A well-trained regiment will go through and emerge from a wood in almost as complete order as it would move across the open; a partially trained one would never come out at all, except perhaps on the wrong side of it, and similarly with minor obstacles. Smokeless powder is also claimed as an advantage, and so it may be if the defenders happen to be the best troops, for they well understand how to conceal themselves, and their opponents have not the trained intelligence to know *where to look*, which makes all the difference. Our numerous villages, too, are spoken of as tactical points of support, but the new high-explosive shells and the small-bore hardened bullets have robbed them of almost all the value they once possessed.

The poisonous fumes of a melinite shell bursting in a house would render the interior untenable, and the ordinary brick-and-a-half structures of our modern jerry builders would be cut through by a few volleys of modern musketry almost like cardboard.

If ever the emergency does arise and we are called on to fight either French or Russians, I believe our best policy will be to march boldly to meet them. We may not—indeed, in England we are pretty certain to have neither numbers, weapons, nor training equal to those of our enemy, but we shall always have soldiers in all grades from highest to lowest capable of forming bold resolves and acting on them, and it will be better policy to adopt a form which gives these qualities their fullest scope, than to hamper them with the bonds in which the defensive inevitably binds those who put their faith in it.

One word more with regard to the duration of the artillery duel. The attacking artillery always starts with the advantage of being able to open fire from an unexpected direction, and from points of its own choosing, which cannot well be foreseen by the enemy, who, though he may know the distance in yards, still has to "range" his guns. The assailant has to "range" too, but starts with the advantage of the first shot, which means a good deal. He may also,, if skilfully handled, thoroughly disconcert all the defenders' arrangements by assailing him from unexpected directions in which previously constructed entrenchments may hinder his replying; this has frequently happened, notably at Königgrätz.

With equally well trained artilleries in a duel between two batteries on one side against one on the other, whilst the latter knocks one gun out of action the former will destroy two obviously. It will then be a case of four guns versus eleven, and while the four are disabling one of the eleven, the eleven will probably smash up three, and I leave it to the reader how long one gun would maintain the struggle against ten. This is what I meant by referring to the "cumulative" action of numbers.

There remains, therefore, only the question of the possibility of passing one line of guns through another, and that appears to me to present but little difficulty. The batteries first in action having been warned" to leave sufficient intervals between themselves to permit of the passage of the second line, as the latter approach the former open a rapid fire with common shell. No smoke now interferes with the movement of the advancing artillery, but the enemy's front is completely swathed in the smoke-screen of the bursting shells, and the fire is maintained for some minutes till it is seen that the advancing line has halted, and it is in action. The range is given to the new arrivals as they pass through the firing line, and they can deduct the distance traversed by counting the stride of their horses—some one man at least per battery would keep his head well enough to do this—and thus they would have a sufficient guide to open fire with shrapnel at once, on unlimbering, within the limit of the short bracket.

If it is urged that such movements are too complicated and too long for execution, my answer is that the artillery should be trained to such a pitch that they do not find any difficulty in them. The Germans could certainly answer these requirements, and what they can do we can do also and a good deal better. As for the distance, that depends on the weight behind the trains, and if that is too great, then here we have very good reason for reducing it. A 12-pounder in action is a very good gun, but a 9-pounder in the right place, at the right time, is better than many 12-pounders still toiling away in the rear when they are urgently wanted in front.

The Prussian Cavalry in 1815

The following is a *précis* of the special writings on cavalry by General von der Marwitz. This first pamphlet was written as an explanatory justification of the apparent harshness with which Blücher had expressed himself in his report of the fighting around Ligny, Wavre, and Waterloo as to the part specially played by the cavalry, a report which was bitterly resented by most of the men concerned, as implying cowardice on their part; indeed, one of the commanders of a Volunteer Cavalry brigade is said to have challenged Blücher to single combat—a challenge which was treated with the contempt it deserved.

The aggrieved parties claimed to have shown courage and devotion in their endeavours to accomplish their duty, and Von der Marwitz grants that they did so, but proceeds to point out that courage and devotion without skill are of little value, and then proceeds to show why the necessary skill was wanting; and the reasons he gives are so sound and of such universal application that they have as much interest for us today as at the time they were written.

His first question, "What are the elements which make an efficient cavalry?" and his second, "Were these elements in existence in the Prussian horse of that day?"

These elements are partly moral, partly physical in principle; they are analogous to those which constitute the strength of a good infantry, but their application is infinitely more complicated, because they depend on the cooperation of two living organisms, the rider and the horse. The moral elements are personal courage in the individual, and *esprit de corps* vivifying the whole mass.

The physical ones are soundness and condition combined with 'horsemanship' in the ultimate unit, the horse and his rider, and mobility and precision in all field movements of the whole

PRUSSIAN CAVALRY PURSUIT AFTER GROSS BEEREN

PRUSSIAN CAVALRY COLONEL

Lützow's wild huntsmen

body.

The words of Blücher's report have been taken by the other arms to imply a deficiency of personal courage in the individuals of the arm, but this view is untenable, for the recruits of the cavalry came from the same class as those of the infantry, whose courage nobody questions, and all were equally imbued with the same love of country and desire for revenge. It is ridiculous, therefore, to assume that all the brave men joined the infantry while the cowards elected for the cavalry. The reason for our failure must lie deeper than this, and we will return to it when we have dealt with the other points.

Esprit de corps is a virtue which requires a 'body'—*i. e*, a mass of men in which to manifest itself. Where it exists, it raises the courage of the individual through the confidence he feels in his comrades and the dread of their ridicule if he shows himself unworthy. Honour and shame are more keenly felt by the mass than by the individual, and when, as in the last two years (1813 15), the desire to sacrifice oneself to achieve the liberation of the farther land has inflamed every heart, it can by judicious choice of means be made into an almost irresistible moral force. Were these judicious means adopted in the cavalry arm?

The officers are the representatives of the men, the true pillars on which regimental tradition, which is almost synonymous with *esprit de corps*, rests. If it dies out amongst them, it cannot live long among the lower ranks except in a perverted form—which in time may react most perniciously on the officers, giving rise to a spirit of exclusiveness and regimental self-righteousness which may cause most serious embarrassment to the army leaders by the friction it entails in the execution of orders.

As a consequence, the members of the body of officers must be relatively numerous, so that the seed may take root in them, and the public opinion of the majority be able to compel the obedience of individuals. In a body of from ten to twenty members only a healthy e*sprit de corps* can scarcely exist.

I may note here that the author does not contemplate any such overgrown bodies of officers as the Indian Staff Corps, the Royal Artillery, or Engineers; the limit he has in his mind is evidently from 40 to 60, and not more.

The officers must belong for a considerable time to their regiments, so that they learn to look on the regiment as their home. For a corporate spirit is opposed to the promptings of selfishness, and if men live long together, no personal consideration will induce a man to cut the ties which bind him to his brother officers. But if you wish to destroy this collective spirit, then move your officers about constantly, so that they never have time to form these ties. You may thus evolve men of ambition fit to be leaders, but there will be no regiments in the true sense of the word for them to lead.

The observance of these rules is all the more essential with troops of new formation such as ours have been during the recent wars (1813-15), for when no time has been given for *esprit de corps* to form amongst the men, the officers become its sole supporters.

With regard to the men, the same principles require strong regiments. Better fewer strong regiments formed by the expansion of existing cadres, and inheriting the traditions of their names and colours, than many weak ones formed new from colonel to drummer-boy.

The number of officers in our cavalry regiments is too small—only 23—and that total is rarely maintained. They have been too frequently interchanged, and notably before the commencement of the last campaign whole regiments were denuded of their leaders, who were distributed throughout other ones.

The regiments are in themselves too weak, and the formation of some more by taking a squadron from each and grouping every four of these squadrons to form a new one was a blunder of the worst kind at a time when we were almost in face of the enemy. Hence of all the elements that go to the formation of a true *esprit de corps* not one existed, nor, in the nature of things, could exist in the Prussian cavalry when we last took the field. Of courage and zeal in the individuals there was as much as in any other body of troops, but of the habit of mind which can combine these qualities into a useful whole, and which alone renders the regiments and squadrons reliable tools in the hands of their leaders, there was no trace, and there could not be.

Coming now to the physical qualifications, and taking first the soundness and conditions of man and horse—considered as an indissoluble unit—it is the case that the great majority of

119

our horses were radically unsound. After 1812, when the few remaining suitable horses had either died in Russia or been ruined by overwork, we had to collect an enormous number of animals to reconstruct the cavalry, and these were neither sufficient in number, nor was there even time enough to admit of making suitable choice.

We had, in fact, to take what we could get. Old riding-horses, carriage-horses, cart-horses, whatever the French had left over for us, all these, either already broken-down horses or young untrained ones, had to be mounted by recruits who could not be expected to, and certainly did not, understand how to save their mounts by bringing the strain on the stronger and sounder parts and relieving the weaker ones. In two rapidly conducted campaigns, of which the last took place in winter, the forehands of almost all the remaining horses were ruined. They became so hopelessly stiff in front that one can characterise the whole lot with absolute conviction as hopelessly unsuited for cavalry purposes. Nevertheless, during the few months of intervening peace we received only a very small percentage of remounts, and, as a body, took the field in a most unsatisfactory condition as regards soundness.

As to the usefulness of man and horse combined, the standard was an exceedingly low one, and for the following reasons: Taken together, the usefulness of the unit (man and horse) depends on this, that the man is able to take his horse at any desired pace in any direction and over any ground, and under all conditions to be able to use his weapons with, effect against the enemy. The art by which these purposes are attained, and which on the one hand develops the strength of the rider, and on the other secures that the powers of the animal are made the most of by saving the weaker and working the stronger parts of his frame, is termed horsemanship.

An unbroken horse is useless so long as he remains in that condition, for the purposes above indicated. A rider who does not know how to control the movements of his mount to the extent needful for these purposes is nothing more than an unfortunate surrendered to the uncontrolled impulses of a timid but dangerous beast. Now during late years the art of horsemanship has become extinct in our cavalry. The horses are no longer in the control of their riders. When one wants them to gallop, they bolt; when they are required to stand still, they turn about, because they do not understand what the pressure of the leg should indicate; if one requires them to leave the ranks or pass other horses, they won't do so, or run up against the others—in short, they obey their own untutored instincts instead of the will of their riders.

The young soldier on such a brute is in a truly pitiable state, for he has to submit to the animal's moods without knowing how to control them; compelled to do the best he can, as far as his strength permits, he jobs the poor brute in the mouth, gives it the spur, and at length brings it into a worse state of desperation than he is in himself; for the *aids* he employs are almost always the wrong ones, and only encourage the horse to resist, not to yield himself.

That such a man, entirely occupied with his horse, and carried whither he wotteth not, is in no position to make proper use of his weapons is self-evident. He is, therefore, useless as a cavalry soldier. But this in the main is the condition of our cavalry. I do not say that every man is so helpless, for that is nearly impossible, and if they were so, all hope of improvement would be at an end; but I insist that the majority are so. And though some regiments are better than others, yet as a body they are more or less in the same boat. And as an old and experienced cavalry soldier I say that the art of horsemanship is so far lost that in the whole army there is hardly a single young officer left who understands how to train horse and rider from the beginning upwards.

If we go on at the present rate, then with the last of the old squadron leaders the art will finally disappear. And a new view of the matter has crept in since the time that our cavalry first began to deteriorate, and perhaps it has its origin in this very deterioration. This view, namely, is that horsemanship is unnecessary for cavalry; courage, the reins loose on the horse's neck, and a sharp pair of spurs are the only necessary elements, so alone can one overthrow the enemy.

This idea at once stamps the school from whence it arises, as no cavalry soldier's—a man on a horse who cannot ride will only then succeed in driving his horse into the enemy's ranks by letting go the reins and sticking in his spurs when the horse is either blind with terror and the enemy is close in front, or when it is so fresh with over-feeding and standing in the stall that it runs away from sheer light-heartedness. Under all other conditions, particularly when wearied with the long marches necessary to meet the enemy, it never goes straight for him, but always tries to run away in an arc till its head is turned towards its last night's quarters.

Whoever has ridden in a charge which the enemy attempted to face knows for certain that no single horse of itself ever desires to face the collision, but that rather they all pull up and try to turn away from it. If the charge is to succeed, then the rider must compel his horse to maintain the direction. The French, also shocking horsemen, try to prevent this inevitable tendency by closing the flies so tight that the horses cannot turn round, and advance so slowly that the line cannot open out.

The opponents of horsemanship base their case on the fact that the French, whom they admit to be execrable horsemen, have nevertheless on occasions succeeded, ignoring that it was by this method, and from these isolated occurrences have established a principle without troubling themselves over such details. Strangely enough, though many people will admit their deficiencies and want of skill in other arts, such as dancing, fencing, swimming, and so forth, no one will ever allow that he cannot ride. He may go so far as to confess he is not a school-rider, but he gets out of that by saying that he considers school-riding (*i. e.,* horsemanship) as of no account.

He gets to the place he wants to, and he does not fall off, and that seems to him suffiient. One's eyes tell one that he ought to fall off a dozen times a day if he did not carefully avoid the risks which a cavalryman between his comrades has to take as they come, for it is evident that his legs are in the wrong place to control his horse's movements, and he is entirely at the animal's mercy. Many a horse has been rejected as vicious and untameable by him merely because it refused to stand still when its rider was applying aids to make it go on, and after many disappointments he has perhaps got together three or four animals gentle and long-suffering enough to allow him to do what he likes on their backs, and he is then satisfied—he can ride, not school fashion perhaps, but he can ride.

Such a man forgets that a cavalry soldier cannot choose his own mount, but must be content with what is given him, and that he can never avoid the opportunities of falling off that present themselves, but must at all times be ready to go where he is ordered on the horse provided for him.

The horse is a living machine which the rider controls at his will; but just as little as a machine can go of itself, but is at all times dependent on the knowledge of the man who moves the starting levers, so little also can a horse be managed by a man not taught to manage it.

From the above it is clear that our cavalry has decayed from two reasons; first, because the horses were not trained or had become broken down in the service; secondly, because our men could not have ridden then in any case.

Next comes skill in field movements. Perhaps, after what has been said above, it may seem unnecessary to enlarge on this point, for how can a cavalry possess skill in combined movements when the individuals are in themselves useless; but it will throw additional light on the subject if we investigate a little the conditions which the field movement of a good cavalry ought to satisfy.

These conditions are, briefly stated, mobility and vehemence in the charge. If these things were not in themselves desirable, then why should one go to the expense and trouble of forming cavalry at all?

But the two conditions are in themselves contradictory. Mobility is most easily obtained with light men on small active horses, vehemence in the charge by men on powerful upstanding ones, and you cannot easily combine the two. If nature had made all men of one weight, and all horses the same size, such a combination might be possible, but since men and horses are not all cast in the same mould, the best way out of the difficulty is to sort them out in at least two (possibly three) different classes of cavalry—light, heavy, and medium—and give to each its special drill regulation, which should develop the pace and vehemence of the heavy branch to the utmost, and the celerity and power of overcoming all obstacles in the light cavalry also to its extreme limit.

A cavalry neither vehement in shock nor rapid in its movements is practically useless; it would be better to spend the money they cost on infantry only, for the foot soldier is more independent. He has no horse to get hungry, sick, or lame, and as long as his strength holds out no obstacle is altogether insuperable to him, whereas external influences constantly impede the horseman. If, therefore, I sacrifice these two advantages of mobility, and accustom my heavy cavalry to charge only at a walk or trot, as the French do, or my light cavalry to find an insuperable hindrance in every ditch and fence they meet with, I should do better without them altogether, preserving only a few mounted men to carry orders and do a little perfunctory reconnoitring.

But how will it fare with me in a war with an enemy who possesses a numerous and determined cavalry, rapid and quick in manoeuvre, and I meet him in an open country? History gives the answer, and that is a very unfavourable one. Cavalry, therefore, is essential, and if essential, then it follows that it must be trained so as to develop those points in which it is superior to the infantry to the highest limit possible: the light cavalry, specially in rapidity of movement across country independently; the heavy, in pace and vehemence of shock.

Rapidity of movement is, however, not merely a question of reckless galloping about; such a course only ruins the horse by uselessly wasting its strength. The true art consists in handling the horse in such a manner as to save him as much as is consistent with the object to be attained, and next in a drill which permits of a desired movement being executed in the least time and by the shortest line. The vehement charge, the special province of heavy cavalry, requires the fulfilment of two conditions—pace and closed flies, the latter with the special object of uniting by the pressure inwards the momentum of the individuals into that of the mass.

Our cavalry is incapable of either form of action; it can neither get about nor charge boot to boot. Its drill regulations are modelled on those of the infantry. Common sense would indicate, with arms having such widely different methods of action, the same form of drill cannot possibly be common to both. Things have got to such a pass that a regiment of infantry now manoeuvres faster than one of cavalry. Those who do not believe that our cavalry is nowadays slow, because they adopt the French as a standard, should look back twenty-six years or so, and remember what our drill used to be when the tradition of Seydlitz's days was still with us. Compare even the drill of the Saxon and Bavarian horse with the miserable performances of our own.

Our charges are ridden too loose. This dates from the time when on the drill-ground charges began to be judged from the flank instead of from the front. The criterion of good charging is now held to be perfect dressing and with properly closed files. Perfect dressing is only possible with the most perfectly trained men and horses, which we no longer possess. Since the inspectors would have it so, it became the custom to open the files, so that now one may see even a *cuirassier* regiment charge with a horse's breadth between the files, and hence it has happened to us that we have been overthrown in the charge by the worst cavalry in the world, which possesses only this one qualification of sticking to one another knee to knee at a trot or walk.

Formerly charges were only judged from the front. If they came on fast and well closed up, they were good; no one troubled, even if a squadron did forge a little ahead. We must go back to that if we intend to do anything, and in this connection I may add that, if we do so, we must also reintroduce the old long, stiff jack-boot, for without them no man could endure the pressure in a charge ridden closed as it used to be.

It is the greatest conceivable shame to us that we should have allowed such indifferent horsemen as the French to obtain a temporary superiority over us. But it will be a worse error still if we try to regenerate ourselves by copying their methods. We must meet their closed advance at a trot, with closed files at a gallop, and, once for all, make it a rule to attack them in flank and rear with our light horsemen. This is a manoeuvre which no enemy whose men are not complete masters of their horses can withstand, also one which cannot successively be carried out by a cavalry which fails to fulfil this condition.

With a little practice, and backed by our good infantry, we shall always be a match for the French; but where should we be in a war on the plains of Poland against the numerous light cavalry of Russia, which in its way possesses many excellent points. But even the Russians cannot serve as our standard of excellence, for there is yet another cavalry, the Turkish, against which they have never been able to make head. The excellence of the Turks consists in their perfect individual mastery over their horses, and the use of their weapons in single combat.

In conclusion then, I will recapitulate the essential joints which must not be disregarded if we are again to occupy our former pre-eminence.

1. Stronger regiments.

2. More officers to the regiment, a consequence of No. 1.

3. Transfers to be made as seldom as possible.

4. Better horses.

5. Revival of the art of horsemanship.

6. A more rapid system of field movements, with a different drill for heavy and light cavalries.

These points, if duly attended to, would give us the machines capable of doing what we require, but only on condition that the men and officers are animated with the proper spirit; and that can only be the case when both are treated in a manner to raise their pride in the performance of their duties.

Those who are interested in this question of cavalry efficiency, which lies at the root of all true appreciation of combined tactics, will do well to refer to the work of the late General Michel, R. A., which confirms the above in a very marked manner, and deals particularly with the inferiority of the French cavalry in the Napoleonic era as compared with our own.

The book is now very difficult to get, but about June, 1890, I wrote a summary of his views, under the title *Napoleon's Cavalry*, which may still be in existence and more accessible.

In the main, the reform of the Prussian cavalry has followed the lines above indicated, though Von der Marwitz would probably consider the regiments as still too weak—they are now five squadrons with 30 officers—he would perhaps prefer the Austrian system of six squadrons and a strong *dépôt*. But as regards the separation of light and heavy cavalries by two distinct regulations, no one has followed his suggestion, and yet it seems to me that much is to be said for it. For charging one wants the most powerful horses and the tallest (or, at least, the strongest) men, but such horses are incapable of standing the fatigues of outpost duty to the same extent as the smaller and more active ones of the light cavalry.

Without raising the old question of cavalry versus infantry, it must be evident that the days of cavalry versus cavalry are by no means at an end. In such conflicts nothing has changed since the days of

Cromwell; swords and lances are as powerless today to pierce a *cuirass* as they were then. A *cuirass* has many drawbacks—possibly a coat of mail might be far better; its weight would be about seven pounds, which could be easily taken off the existing saddles without impairing their efficiency—indeed, I would undertake to get a whole stone off them; and since heavy cavalry should not be required to go on outpost duty, there is no valid reason why every *cuirassier* should carry a carbine and ammunition, only perhaps a dozen per troop being served out to the lighter men, so as to equalize the weight on the horses.

The onset of such cavalry should be irresistible, and in a *mêlée* these mail-clad men able to give their whole attention to the work of killing, and protected against all cuts and points of the enemy, would, I take it, make short work of any horseman in Europe. As it is the "heavy" is practically useless. After turn and turn about at the outposts with the light, he reaches the field with his horse so reduced in condition that, owing to want of speed, he is for shock purposes no better than the light cavalry on fresher horses, and in the *mêlée* itself his length of arm is of no avail, for men are locked too closely to be able to take advantage of it, and the smaller man with the shorter sword would have altogether the best of it.

General Von der Marwitz's Second Cavalry Pamphlet

This pamphlet, written in 1816, gave rise to much discussion in the Prussian Army, and the general set himself to work in the following year to answer the objections raised, and in doing so he gives a far better insight into the condition of things than any other writer with whom I am acquainted. He states:

It was the object of my previous essay to search out the cause of the decay of our cavalry to the roots, and thus lay bare the true evils which we must attack if it is to be regenerated. I therefore examined the true nature of the arm, both from the physical and moral standpoint, and under each head investigated the influence of these factors on the mass and on the individual: and in the following lines I purpose to stick to the same arrangement, and finally to add a few words as to the employment of cavalry.

On the subject of *esprit de corps,* it has been objected that this quality has existed, and can originate in small bodies as well as large ones. The case of our celebrated old 'Black Hussars' before Jena is quoted as in point, which regiment was so much split up in detachments that some of the officers had never met the whole of their comrades during their service, and yet notoriously the *esprit de corps* of the whole was exceptionally developed and maintained. Our present small regiments, it is said, are a parallel case, and means must exist which would evolve an equally satisfactory condition of things.

This instance, properly understood, strengthens my case, and does not undermine it. But we must first distinguish between the origin of a sentiment and its maintenance. This regiment was originally a strong corps of 65 officers and 1,500 men, and its *esprit de corps* had originated during many successive years of a peculiarly arduous war-time, in which the regiment again and again distinguished itself, and during all this period the regiment worked together.

When then at a subsequent date it was split up in detachments, the sentiment was already there, and propagated itself onward. But it could never have originated under these altered circumstances. But whence are our new regiments to draw this inspiration? Some of them have done nothing of a nature to call this feeling into being; in others, more fortunate, the men who performed these deeds have been transferred to other corps, and will be so again. In the former case the sentiment cannot exist, in the latter it disappears almost as soon as it is created.

If the present condition of things is to remain with us, I see only one way out of the difficulty—namely, to transfer the sentiment of the corps to the branch of the arm; mass the cuirassiers, dragoons, and hussars each in separate stations, allow no transfers from one to another, and teach a man to have pride in being a *cuirassier* or hussar, instead of being only a member of such and such a regiment.

Once for all, I must guard myself from misinterpretation. I have never said that *esprit de corps* is a necessary product of massing men together, but only that it can only originate in a mass. Take a mass of men and treat them in a manner to offend their pride, change them from pillar to post, make the present a source of bitterness to them, and rob them of all hope in the future, and you may be certain, not only that no such plant will spring into being from such a soil, but also, if it already exists, it will soon wither and die.

With reference to the physical utility of the arm, and its connection with the art of horsemanship, it has been urged that it will be necessary to fix the limits beyond which the study of the art shall not be pursued; otherwise we shall fall into the errors which prevailed before 1806, and in care for the individual lose sight of the efficiency of the whole.

My answer to this is that, in the first place, so soon as you set a limit to art of any kind, you conventionalise it, and, *ipso facto*, it ceases to be. At most the shadow of a trade remains. Free play of all powers, bodily and mental, are necessary for the artists, and to very few is it given to excel. The masses remain always far behind and learn at most the bare essentials. Say that no one shall pass the boundary, and all emulation ceases; by degrees the standard of excellence is lost, and the average of the whole deteriorates. The gifts that go to the making of a perfect horseman are far too rare to cause anxiety, lest the world become too full of them, and more particularly so at the present moment, when the question for us is—how to get out of the slough in which we are walking, and when in the whole army there are probably not 50 real horsemen left to us. If, however, it should come to pass, which I fervently hope, but do not expect, that within a few years our cavalry should attain too high a standard of individual horsemanship, then nothing is easier than to stop it, by making the regiments do more drill and route marching, so that they will no longer have time to excel.

Secondly, it is not the case that good horsemanship was so universally disseminated before 1806 as is usually supposed, and I am in a position to show that it neither was nor could be so.

The regiment of *Gens-d'armes*, in which I served for thirteen years, was by general consent the one in which individual horsemanship was carried to the highest pitch; so what I can prove with regard to this one will apply with fair accuracy to all.

Our strength was 10 companies, each company, without counting non-commissioned officers, consisted of 66 privates, of whom half were on furlough, and were only called up for the drill season, which lasted from the 16th of March to the 23rd of May, nine weeks in all. Out of these nine weeks, only three were allotted to individual riding in the school, and each man rode for an hour a day, or 18 hours in all. It must be admitted that 18 hours is not too much for a man who for the rest of the year was engaged at his trade in the fields or workshops.

Then for three weeks, to the time of the 'special review,' the regiment went out to drill on alternate days, so that the man again mounted his horse 9 times. After the 'special review,' a number of the men were again sent on furlough, only enough being retained to enable us to go out to drill with 24 files per company, and these few men again got on their horses 9 times in all. In the autumn we had another three weeks' drill, but with only 20 files per company, and no individual riding at all.

Hence it follows that at the outside no furlough man had more than 18 hours' riding drill, and only mounted his horse for drill in the ranks 27 times, and no one who knows what the difficulties of the matter are will complain that this is too much time to bestow on such an important matter.

But, it may be asked. How was it with the remaining 33 duty men—surely they must have all been perfect centaurs? Unfortunately, from these we must deduct the recruits and *freiwachters* (those were men struck off all duties and allowed to work in the town at their trades). There were 10 of the latter allowed by regulation, and as a body they rode worse than the men on furlough, for they only paraded when the regiment went out at its full strength, and never went to riding drill at all. Of recruits there would be an average of 8 annually, and since two years is the least time in which to make a horsemen, there were 16 at a time undergoing their training. So that of the 33 men only 7 remain from whom one could with reason expect that they should ride perfectly.

Of horses, each company had 75, and received every year 8 remounts. As they were very young, they could not be put in the ranks under three or four years; 24 must therefore, be subtracted from the available strength. But amongst the horses passed by the riding master there are always some which, owing to want of shape, weakness, or trifling defects of soundness, can never be regarded as perfectly trained. Take these at a seventh of the whole, and in this case we must deduct another 10. Finally, a certain number had to be set apart for the use of the recruits, and these it was impossible to train perfectly, for they passed from the hands of one beginner to another, and as every recruit had to ride every day, we must deduct 2 horses for each, or in all 16 horses; so that for the whole company there were necessarily 66 partly trained horses, and there could only be 9 thoroughly broken charges. Is this overdriving the art, when by no possibility could there be more than 7 trained horsemen out of 66, and only 9 thoroughly broken horses out of 75?

When this art is the one mainspring of the efficiency of the whole arm, with less we could not have got along at all. The whole noise has been raised because, when anyone saw a selected detachment ride in the school, he was astonished at their performances, and easily came to the false conclusion that the whole regiment had attained the same degree of skill.

I would stop here for a minute to ask whether this remark does not apply with some force to the estimate amateurs are apt to form of the horsemanship of our cavalry when they see the performances of our specially selected and carefully trained men at the Agricultural Hall and similar places. As long as the efficiency of the regiment is all that a competent inspector general says it should be, there is no ground of complaint, for the best regiment will turn out the best picked riders; but when, as sometimes happens, the whole routine of an under-horsed regiment is sacrificed in order to make a show before the public, even with the laudable object of attracting recruits, I consider it is time for some capable critic to step in and show the injury actually done to the service.

Again it has been brought forward against the individual training of our cavalry that the performances of our *Landwehr* cavalry showed that one could do very well without this thorough training. They were quickly shown the essentials, and that had sufficed for the purpose. To this objection I reply that, when the *Landwehr* was first formed, we had two mighty moral assistants: first, the universal hatred of French domination; second, a certain number of experienced cavalry officers who really understood the essentials of the duties and of horsemanship, and who were in a position to decide what things were of first necessity, and to teach only these.

The first of these factors is unlikely to occur again, and as for the second, horsemanship is so far a forgotten art that not all the good will in the world, if untutored, will avail anything.

"I see no other means except to form a central riding establishment, in which horsemanship and the theory and practice of bitting shall be taught, and to which officers from every regiment in the service will be sent to learn in order hereafter to teach his subordinates. And then, when the school has had time to exercise due influence, every officer who cannot ride shall be relegated to the infantry.

This could not hurt the feelings of the latter, for it is no disgrace not to be able to ride, and a very bad man on a horse may be a very good one on his feet.

Coming now to the question of drill, it has been objected that I speak only of the charge, which, after all, is not the only form of employment for the cavalry; a more important point is the way in which reconnaissance and outpost duties are performed.

If I really failed to express myself clearly on this head, it is, I admit, a mistake, and I will at once endeavour to correct it. My intention was certainly not to underrate the service of the light cavalry, but only to insist that there should be two distinct forms of drill and training for light and heavy, suited to the requirements of each. What I mean may be freely stated thus. Heavy cavalry exists for the purpose of developing vehemence and momentum in the attack; light cavalry, to utilise to the utmost the speed and dexterity of horse and rider.

It stands to reason, therefore, that this difference should be taken into account in the training of the two types.

The charge of heavy cavalry cannot be ridden too close or too fast. The horse should, therefore, not be made too susceptible to the pressure of the leg, for it must not only endure the pressure of the files on one another, but also resist it. It must not be thrown too much on its haunches, nor should it be too easy to strike off in a gallop, for this last not only irritates its comrades on either hand, but leads to crowding and consequent confusion. The rider must certainly have his mount under control, but the main points to insist on are riding straight to the front and the compact closing of the flies.

Light cavalry cannot be too fast in their movements. Their horses must, therefore, have light mouths, and yield readily to the pressure of the leg. They must also be thoroughly trained to the gallop, in perfect balance, so that all the forces of the animal are collected and at the disposal of the rider. Then it will combine endurance at speed with the power of jumping and scrambling up or down nasty slopes, in the highest possible manner. For the same reasons, the rider must not only thoroughly understand the principles of horsemanship, but his judgment must be trained to understand how to save his horse to the utmost, and then, in case of necessity, to get the last ounce possible out of him.

These points must underlie the training of the whole. The heavy cavalry remains in all movements compactly closed, and whoever allows himself to be squeezed out of the ranks should be punished. But at the same time they must be very steady. Therefore they should manoeuvre, as a rule,, at a long roomy trot, carrying them rapidly over the ground, particularly in de-

133

ployments. In moving off for the charge, too, they should start at a trot, and the greatest care must be taken before sounding the 'march' that all horses are dead square to the front and properly closed up. Also, since the habit of loose riding has crept in, the following point deserves special attention: the regulation prescribes that 'the pressure from the directing flank should be given way to, that from the reverse one resisted,' also 'the squadron intervals are to be maintained during the charge.' Now, what happens every time?"

No horse ever goes quite so dead straight to its front that now and again deviations do not occur. The directing flank moves direct on its object, and must not be crowded off; hence all the deviations tend towards the reverse one. In a few moments the man on the reverse flank begins to yield to the culminating pressure, and the squadron's interval is decreased. As this is not allowed, the next squadron gives way too, and the next, so that after a few hundred yards, when the 'halt' is sounded, the whole force is all over the place; or, if it is on active service, the properly closed opponent crashes right through us. For this I see only one corrective—that the centre file of the squadron should always direct.

After the long roomy trot with which the attack is commenced, the gallop is sounded some 300 paces from the enemy, and the charge at 60 paces. The 'halt' should never be commanded with the voice, but always sounded (nowadays, (as at time of first publication), in Germany it is never sounded at all, but only the 'disperse' and 'rally'), and no blame must attach to any one if one squadron is a little in front of the other; but if the files have been loosened, then the men must be scolded, and if necessary, punished.

The light cavalry must keep their horses in hand, and therefore ride either a short collected trot or gallop. They must be able to execute all evolutions at a gallop; they should not charge with the files too close, but always have room to wheel up to a flank in a column of troops to meet or make a flank attack, and they must devote more time to reconnaissance and outpost duties than to anything else.

The characteristic of the heavy cavalry must be to suffer no opposition, but to go straight for the enemy wherever they meet him, and ride him down by pace and weight; therefore they must never be brought up till actually wanted, and never used in pursuit, which duty after a successful charge is taken up by the light. The moment the charge is over, they must rally to be ready for a new one should that become necessary.

The light, on the other hand, should find their chief strength in manoeuvre, and never charge except when an opening is given. They must be able to play with the enemy for hours together, not hesitating to retreat to lure him on; but once the chance is given, they must charge home and pursue to the last breath of their horses.

The heavy cavalry must possess an even Quixotic faith in their power, which it will be the special province of their leader to keep within bounds; the light, on the other hand, must pride itself on its pace, cleverness, and individualism.

The remainder of the pamphlet may be dealt with more rapidly, for much no longer applies to present conditions.

Heavy cavalry, according to the author, must be cuirassed for the same reason I gave in the concluding lines of my last letter. The front rank should be armed with lances, but of a longer and better balanced pattern than existing ones, so that when brought to the charge the points should project a clear four feet in front of the horses' heads. The rear rank, on the other hand, and all light cavalry, should have swords only.

The necessity for large bodies of cavalry being collected in camps of exercise annually is also strongly insisted on.

And it is curious to find this man of so many years' war experience recommending that heavy cavalry should be trained occasionally to charge in *close* column. He admits all the drawbacks, but urges that in the supreme moment, when success must be won at any cost, the certainty of the result justifies the risk, provided the men have been previously trained to feel nothing unusual in such a course, and the description he gives of such a column breaking through and shattering all resistance reminds one of the instance quoted in James Skinner's memoirs of the charge of 10,000 Khattore horse against a brigade of regular Mahratta infantry in the Battle of Jeypore. The brigade formed square eight deep to met them, and with perfect steadiness reserved their fire till the cavalry were within 100 paces or so, but it hardly checked the onslaught; the mass swept over the whole brigade, and out of some 8,000 men, not 200 were known to have survived.

In conclusion, let me quote a scolding Frederick the Great gave to his cavalry in his latter years at Potsdam. He sent for all the officers after a manoeuvre day, and addressed them somewhat as follows:

Gentlemen, I am entirely dissatisfied with the cavalry; the regiments are completely out of hand, there is no accuracy in their movements, no solidity and no order. The men ride like tailors. I beg that this may not occur again, and that each of you will pay more attention to his duty, more particularly to the horsemanship.

But I know how things go on. The captains think only of making money out of the squadron, and the lieutenants, how to get the most leave. You think I am not up to your dodges, but I know them all, and will recapitulate them. Tomorrow, when you start on your march back to your garrison, before you are 10 miles on the way, the squadron commander will ask the sergeant-major whether any of the men live in the vicinity, and the sergeant-major will reply: 'Yes sir, there is so and so, and so and so live quite close to here, and would be glad to go on furlough.' 'Very well, then,' the captain will say, 'we can save their pay. Send the names in to me tonight, and they shall all have it,' and so it goes on every march. The lieutenants get leave to visit their friends, and the captain arrives at his garrison with half his squadron leading the horses of the other half, like a band of disreputable Cossacks.

Then, when the season for riding drills comes on, the captain sends for the sergeant-major and says: 'I have an appointment this morning at so and so, and must get away early; tell the first lieutenant to take the rides. So the sergeant-major goes to the first lieutenant and gives him the message, and the latter says: 'What! the captain is away? then I am off hunting; tell the second lieutenant to take the men.' And the second lieutenant, who is probably still in his bed, says: 'What! both of them gone? then I will stay where I am; I was up till 3 this morning at a dance; tell the cornet I am ill, and he must take the ride.' And the cornet says: 'Look here, sergeant-major, what is the good of my standing out there in the cold? You know all about it much better than I do; you go and take the ride,' and so it goes on: and what must be the end of it all? What can I do with such cavalry before the enemy? I tell you, I think so much of the importance of your arm that I expect more from a lieutenant of cavalry than from a major of infantry.

When I visit the outposts, I expect every subaltern in charge of a picket to be able to tell me exactly all about the ground for five miles round, and to be able to make a legible sketch of it."

(Frederick's standard was, however, not so high as that of our present examiners, and some of his own topographical work, republished recently in facsimile, would certainly have entailed his failure in C. and D.)

If I send him on a patrol, he must be able to tell me exactly where and how strong the enemy is and how best to get at him; what the roads are like, and whether I can move guns by them, etc., and when the time for the charge arrives, I expect you to seize the opportunity and to act at once without waiting for orders, which always come too late. Now, march your regiments home, and don't let me have to speak like this again.

The Berlin-Vienna Race

An interesting lecture read before the Berlin Military Society by Lieutenant von Reitzenstein, the winner on the German side in the great long-distance race, has just been published. As it contains some valuable hints on the preparation of horses for great endurance, and removes many false impressions prevailing in England as to the race itself, I purpose to give a tolerably complete summary of the work. Reitzenstein is a well-known gentleman rider in Germany, and it is worth noticing that he did not enter his horse for the competition considering it as a sporting event, but simply and solely as an experiment of sufficient military interest to justify him and his comrades to call on their horses and themselves for the very utmost exertions. Before starting, he reasoned the matter out as follows:

In every autumn manoeuvre, to say nothing of war, cases of two consecutive bivouacs occur which entail two nights and three days with very little rest for the horses, especially for those on outpost and patrols, and all the time they are carrying full marching order kit. It is certain therefore that for so long horses can get on without very much rest. The question is. How far in that time will a suitably selected animal under a light weight succeed in travelling, and what pace will cover most ground? The nerves of the horse's stomach—*i e.,* its digestive powers—are, it is known, less strained by uniform exertion than by the excitement created by rapid movement; therefore to cover the most ground in the given time a uniform steady pace, maintained for the longest possible period, promised the best results. It is better to shorten the periods of rest than to force the pace betweenwhiles and let the animal rest in the stable longer, where he would only get stiff.

THE BERLIN–VIENNA RACE

The most difficult point was to find a suitable horse. He decided to look out for a thoroughbred hunter, and at last heard of one standing in Ghent (Belgium), and set off at once to see it. He found it exactly what he wanted—a thoroughbred mare, 15-3, with magnificent shoulders, well coupled, and good quarters; unfortunately, the animal was suffering from a sore back, but he had only a single day before sending in the name of the horse he meant to ride, and decided to take it as it was. The mare was ten years old, no pedigree available, and he bought her for £80, and christened her "Lippspringe," after a village near his garrison. Subsequently he succeeded in tracing her origin; her name is entered in the English stud-book as *Otation*, brown mare, 1882, by *Siderolite* out of *Gyration*.

She had belonged to an English officer, and had been sold at Tattersall's and sent to Belgium, three years ago. It would be interesting to ascertain what price she fetched, and who the officer was who had owned her. As he did not wish to take leave during the manoeuvres, all the training and preparation had to be undertaken on the march. The mare reached her new quarters on the 3rd of September, and it was soon discovered that she would not stand grooming, and generally was troublesome in the stable.

> I had been worrying a good deal about her unusually low price, wondering what way she would astonish me, and this discovery relieved me. For the usual grooming I substituted washing in lukewarm water and drying with flannels; this soothed her, and she soon became quite gentle. From this period I practically never let her out of my sight, fed her myself, and gave up all my spare time to study her character; in about fourteen days we were on such good terms that she followed me about like a dog, even in the darkness. During the whole ride to Vienna I never led her by the bridle, but walked or ran by her side, taking hold of her mane when trotting downhill.

In consequence of the sore back he used a well-fitting military saddle without blanket or *numnah*; this relieved the sore, of all pressure, and with the aid of mercurial ointment she was all well again in three weeks.

The question of shoeing gave much cause for anxiety, as on the rocky roads over the mountains the danger of a bruised frog was considerable; so he decided to place a leather plate under the shoe, stuffing the space between the leather and the frog with tow smeared with tar.

After a few days the mare went tender in front. There was no heat in the foot, and after a day or two she went better, but still somewhat shorter than seemed normal. However, he decided not to alter the shoeing till he had seen the chief veterinary authority in Berlin. No special preparation to put on muscle was undertaken; he rode her with the troops on a couple of days, and generally took her on the hard roads for a few hours every afternoon for exercise, at the same time endeavouring to get her head in a better position and improve her balance. By experiment he settled on an average speed of 1,100 yards in 4 minutes as most suitable to her build, and she kept this pace up regularly for 20 miles without walking. Her normal trot was much faster, left to herself she covered the 1,100 yards in 2.2 minutes, but this was too much for the purpose—neither heart nor lungs could stand the strain of such exertion for long.

He returns to this point (the importance of saving the internal organs in order to obtain the best results in competitions of this kind) again, and attributes most of the deaths from colic which occurred on the road to neglect of this principle. They rode too fast between the halts, and fed and watered without allowing sufficient time for the internal organs to cool down: judging only by the external signs of cooling, whereas the real point is the gradual return to their normal condition of the blood-vessels and nerves congested or excited by exertion and hidden from sight within the animal itself. This seems to me a point worth bringing out.

It is altogether a different matter, when distances have to be covered so great that pauses for food must necessarily be intercalated, from what it is when the distance,, though great, can yet be done without a halt for feeding. Then one can force the pace, for the duration of the journey is shortened, and there is ample time to cool down on arrival.

Having made friends with his horse, he next tried an experimental trip of 200 kilometres, say 125 miles. Starting at 8 a. m. he covered 50 kilometres and fed the mare with a little bread and lukewarm water, then completed the first 100 kilometres, rested 3 hours and fed with oats, and at night rode the remaining 100 kilometres straight off, reaching his quarters at 3 a. m. In the afternoon he took the mare out again for another 50 kilometres, and found her fresh and strong and appetite excellent. This test satisfied him, and for the remainder of the time he fed her up and kept her in good condition. She used to eat 24 pounds of oats a day, with bran and beans. She was also habituated to eat bread made of crushed oats, maize, and eggs.

On the 24th of September they started for Berlin; next morning, in shunting, the horse-box was driven against the stops, and the mare violently flung against the timbers, inflicting a considerable flesh-wound in the forehead, and though not lame, yet in the afternoon she refused her food, and the veterinary surgeon established slight concussion of the brain with headache. This was only four days before the start. Fortunately, she recovered sufficiently, but the accident must have somewhat interfered with her chances.

Meanwhile, after consultation with the chief veterinary surgeon, the shoes were taken off, and then it was discovered that sand and dirt had worked in under the leather and formed a hard-cake—which accounted for the tenderness. She was now reshod with mild steel shoes of ordinary pattern. These answered excellently, but it is worthy of note that the hind shoes wore down markedly more than the fore ones; this is probably accounted for by the tendency to trail the hind legs when fatigued. Curiously, he forgets to inform us what his actual weight was. I believe about 168 pounds, saddle included, judging by his appearance.

He rode on a light Hungarian saddle, without *numnah*, apparently without panels also, but the point is not quite clearly given; stirrups of aluminum, which saved nearly a couple of pounds. To the right stirrup a cyclist's lantern hung on a spring, to break the concussion, was attached, which answered fairly well. For bridle the ordinary military pattern with hooks arranged to hang the curb on. so as to save time in feeding, etc. On the saddle he carried a small haversack and two shoe-cases. The haversack contained 2 pounds of crushed oats made into bread, referred to above, a small flask of brandy, some Carlsbad salts, some salicylic cotton-wool for bandages, a bandage of gauze, some collodion, and a little tallow and powdered salicylic acid—as an antiseptic. The Carlsbad salts were used to promote digestion and given in every feed.

In the shoe-cases, besides two reserve shoes, were a small hammer and wrench—he had previously gone through a farrier's course and was a fair hand at shoeing a horse; fortunately so, for the second night he had to apply his knowledge. A small sponge, for washing out the nostrils and cooling the head, completed his equipment. His spurs were strapped to the saddle in front, and only used in the last 15 miles; he carried no whip. The hind legs had two brushing stockings lined with smooth leather to prevent caking. His watch was attached to the headstall between the horse's ears. He found this better in daytime than the usual wrist attachment. He sent no grooms on in front, as he decided to regulate his halts by the condition of the horse alone.

Want of time prevented a previous reconnaissance of the road. The study of the staff maps had to suffice, and he admits that from them he had derived a tolerably false impression of the gradients; the scale 1/100000 is too small. In consequence of the accident to the horse above referred to, at the last moment he altered his plans somewhat, and thereby lost a certain amount of time; over the mountains, too, better knowledge of the country might have saved him perhaps an hour and a half. A cyclist from Berlin offered his services to accompany him, and proved very useful in warning people ahead of his arrival. On the morning of the 3rd of October, at 8:50, he started; roads in fair condition, except, through one or two villages where they were paved. At these he dismounted and walked in front of the mare, she following him without the reins.

At 12:25 p. m. reached Baruth, 52 kilometres (31 miles). His cyclist had gone ahead, and ordered the lukewarm water with oatmeal for the horse. For the last ten minutes he walked to cool her, but she showed no fatigue, and was breathing quite normal. Her nostrils were sponged out. She drank her gruel, and they went on to Kalan, 100 kilometres (61 miles); arrived 4 :45 p. m., walked the last 2 miles, and gave the horse more gruel and some hay; for himself took tea with eggs beaten up. At 6 p. m. remounted and rode on, reaching Hoyerswerda, 140 kilometres, at 10 :45 p. m. For the last few miles the stony nature of the road caused some delay; here he dismounted for ten minutes, washed out the mare's nostrils, and went on at once, reaching Klein Welka, 176 kilometres, at 2:30 a. m.

The mare was still fresh and might well have gone on for another two hours, but, owing to her accident, he had broken his original intention of riding on further, and had sent on his groom to meet him there, so he was compelled to stop. The mare was well washed down with warm water, dried, and then some kind of embrocation of a simple nature (not Eillman's or one of Mattei's electricities) well rubbed in. The mare seemed much refreshed, and, after some gruel, ate 14 pounds of oats with Carlsbad salts; the legs were bandaged with wet woollen bandages, and the hoofs cooled by felt pads saturated in water. For himself he had his legs well massaged and rubbed with this embrocation, had a light meal, and rested without sleeping for a couple of hours. After 3 hours, at .5:40 a. m. he rode on. The mare, in spite of her 200 kilometres, say 125 miles, was in excellent condition.

He soon reached the hilly districts, where the gradients were so stiff that his cyclist could no longer keep up, and went round by train to meet him further on. Then, following a local tip, he got into still worse ground and lost much time, and the practical difficulty of accommodating his pace to the slopes began. To trot up hill and walk down, or *vice versa,* would have caused too much delay. He found it best to judge by the feet of the horse, and whether uphill or down, to dismount and run or walk by her side the moment he felt the back muscles relax and the quarters begin to trail. The strain on these muscles and on the spine is the principal point in these long distances. Even if the haunches are still fresh, but the back weary, the impulse forward cannot be properly communicated to the forehand, the connection between the two ceases, and the horse drags itself forward on the forehand alone.

At 4:30 p. m. he reached Weisswasser, 271 kilometres (31 hours, 40 minutes), his horse still fresh; he had 300 kilometres to traverse, and calculated on doing it in 69 hours. His cyclist had met him, having come round the mountains by rail via Dresden, and had warm gruel ready for the mare. After an hour's rest,, at 5 :20 p. m. he rode on to Nimburg, which he reached at 11 p. m.; more gruel and a little bread, for himself a cup of tea, and he went on by New Kolin to Czaslau; but now the roads became abominable, and coming into the valley of the Elbe he found a thick fog. He reached New Kolin about 2 a. m., and in consequence of the fog would have done better to remain there for a few hours' rest, but, unfortunately, he had again broken his good resolution not to send his groom in advance, and the fact that the latter was waiting for him at Czaslau induced him to ride on.

The road was very bad, full of ruts and loose stones, the mare began to stumble, and eventually lost her off hind shoe, which he replaced in 10 minutes, but he had to lead her most of the way, and only reached Czaslau, 19 kilometres from New Kolin, at 6 a. m., seriously lowering his average. He therefore cut down his halt to two hours instead of three, and gave the mare 12 pounds of oats, grooming her as at Klein Welka. For himself he took tea and eggs, and studied the maps. His feet had begun to swell, but he dare not take off his boots, for fear of not getting them on again.

At 8 a. m. he remounted. Though the mare had come 390 kilometres (say 250 miles), she was still fresh and strong. Passing through

Deutschbrod, he learnt that Lieutenant Graf Königsmark and Captain Förster (of the balloon section), who had started two hours before him, were only an hour in front. At Iglau, 415 kilometres, reached at 1:25 p. m.. he halted 15 minutes, giving the mare a bucket of gruel.

Here he learnt that the record of Lieutenant Mikloe, which he already knew, had been beaten by Graf Staremberg, though by how much precisely he could not find out. This is so far of importance, since it was stated at the time in all the papers that the German military *attaché* at Vienna kept him informed of the time of the Austrian competitors by wire, which was not the case. The road beyond Iglau was very indifferent, gradients very steep, and he had to dismount and lead continually. A cold wind also got up and darkness was coming on. Suddenly he heard behind him hoof-beats and Von Förster and Graf Königsmark overtook him; he had passed them whilst resting in a village, he himself having cut a corner, avoiding the village by a by-road. They proposed to rest in Mährisch Budwitz, as they had already come 127 kilometres since their last long halt. As their horses showed signs of fatigue, he proposed they should all go on together—the horses were too tired to risk a long halt.

The more tired the horses become, the more essential to push on and cut down the duration of rest to avoid stiffness setting in. The others agreed, but we determined to give ourselves and our animals a last feed and drink at the next inn. Leaving my cyclist to watch the mare, I went in to get something to eat; I had had nothing since 8 o'clock that morning, and nothing but tea and eggs for the last forty-eight hours. Suddenly I heard coughing outside, and, rushing out, found it was my mare; a thick white foam came from the mouth and nostrils. 'What has happened?' I asked the man. 'Nothing.' he said. 'She has eaten some hay, and as she seemed still thirsty, I gave her some more water.' There was a cold wind blowing. Whether that had chilled her, or whether the man had carelessly given her too cold water, who can say? 'Till this moment I had never left her out of my sight, and now, when double caution was necessary, I had failed to exercise it.

The only chance lay in riding on at once to warm her. I washed out the mouth and nostrils, and remounted. But the cough persisted, and I thought she would come to a dead stand. I dismounted and told Von Förster I should give up, and begged him to ride on. After leading a short time, the cough ceased and the foaming disappeared. I got in the saddle again, and in half an hour she was going as strong as ever. The roads continued very bad, and near Mährisch Budwitz, Graf Königsmark's horse fell over a heap of road metal, cutting both knees; as I passed him, I gave him my bandaging gear, and with Förster again rode on.

At 12 :15 a. m. we reached Znaim. I can no longer recall the incidents of the last four hours; from constantly straining my eyes into the darkness from the fear of falling and the exertion of keeping my weight back to meet a possible stumbling, I was giddy and felt severe pain in the loins. The Austrian officers were ready here to meet us. Warm gruel was prepared for the horses. I had a drink and something to eat, gave the mare some of her own ration of bread steeped in brandy, and after 15 minutes pushed on—80 kilometres (52 miles) and 8 hours to beat the record. My horse was still fresh, and I felt every confidence. As it grew later the fog settled down, and even the lantern proved of little assistance.

The innumerable ruts gave the road a wavy appearance, and now the mare began to stumble repeatedly, only her splendid shoulders saving her from falling. I had carefully studied the map of Znaim, and convinced myself that it was impossible to go wrong, if I stuck to the high road. Unfortunately, the map was wrong and did not show a small bend and fork at the village of 'Grund.' In the fog we took the wrong side of the fork, and, as bad luck would have it, the villages along the wrong road were spaced at equal intervals to those on the right one. There was no one about to ask, and indeed it never occurred to us (myself and the cyclist) that anything was wrong. We came to some steep descents and I dismounted.

Suddenly I became giddy and staggered; fortunately, a house was at hand, and, after some cold water had been poured over my head, I was able to go on. I asked the man where we were, and we then learnt our mistake; instead of only 19 kilometres more to ride, we had still 39 before us. This discovery thoroughly woke me up. I looked at my watch—it was 5:50 a, m. I had only two hours left to beat Staremberg's time. There was therefore not a moment to be lost. I bade *adieu* to Förster and disappeared into the fog. Then I remembered that my brother had told me of a short cut, which, if I could find it, still gave me a chance of winning. If the fog lifted, all would be well; hoping it would, I took the turning. I had to ride across country for a short stretch; the ground was soft, and the mare had to gallop, as it was too deep to trot.

The fog did not lift. I lost my direction and came on a deep mill-stream, hopelessly unfordable. My chance of the prize I saw was gone, and I returned to the main road, having lost 35 minutes. At the first village I halted, gave the mare lukewarm water, the last piece of bread steeped in brandy, and strapped on ray spurs. The short rest had already made the mare stiff,, and she began to stagger. My last chance was to keep her going. I remounted, with a little coaxing; she broke into a trot, and, only using the spurs sufficiently to keep her haunches up, we covered the last seven miles into Floridsdorf. Her pluck and breeding proved decisive here; a meaner animal would have simply declined to move a step further, but she seemed to feel the pride of success, and with a last effort pulled herself together, and passed the finish with head well up and firm regular beat of the hoofs, as the instantaneous photo taken at this moment shows.

Three minutes afterwards she laid down exhausted on the road, where she stayed for some hours; in the afternoon she was taken to her stable. In the night she ate carrots and oats, and on the next day seemed rapidly recovering, but at night fever set in, due to inflammation of the lungs, and to this the poor animal succumbed. No doubt the seed of this inflammation was laid the previous night when she began to cough, and the excess of fatigue, due to the mistake I had made in the roads, just prevented her being taken at once to her stable out of the wind.

In 73 hours. 6 minutes, inclusive of the mistake, the mare had covered 597 kilometres (388 miles); of this two- thirds on bad roads over the mountains. In this time she had rested only 8 hours, and been fed only twice, with about 14 pounds of oats each time. She had had oatmeal gruel as often as it could be conveniently given. As far as Mährisch Budwitz I trotted, changing the diagonal legs alternately, but beyond, owing to the incomplete training of the mare, the near hind foot began to knuckle over, and I was compelled to continue on the near fore-off hind diagonal.

His reflections on the value of the ride as a military experiment practically agree with those already published. With the enormous areas covered by modern armies, officers' patrols are liable to be called on to cover very great distances indeed, and the art will consist in knowing how to do so with the least exertion to the animal. Such a patrol may at any moment end in a ride for life or death, and one's chances of survival depend on the reserve power still left in the horse.

The knowledge that such distances can be traversed by one horse almost without rest must give confidence to every man throughout the army, and enable him to dare to undertake what, in a service in which thirty miles on end is looked on as cruelty to animals, would be regarded as pure foolhardiness. Reitzenstein's performance was actually better than that of the winner; yet, reading his account carefully, it is evident that with better luck and the experience now gained he might have done considerably better. Eliminate the accident to the horse in shunting, the lameness due to bad shoeing, the cough, mistake in the road, and, above all things, reinforce both horse and rider's strength by a knowledge of the Kola nut, and I feel tolerably confident that the same man and horse would have covered the distance in 65 hours.

It is a satisfaction for us that it was an English horse that accomplished this feat, but I regret to say that after seeing the different way these men rode their horses, until the art of horsemanship is better understood in England and India that it is now, I do not believe that she (the mare) would have got over more than three-quarters of the road in the time under the ordinary English rider. The art of getting the utmost out of one's horse on a long distance is one we have yet to learn, and it is precisely we who, as a nation, have the greatest advantage to derive from the knowledge. A ride for life and death from Herat to Kandahar or *vice versa*, the same distance as Berlin to Vienna, is by no means precluded in the present political situation.

General Von Rosenberg's Hints on Recruit Training and Riding

Probably all officers who have had the responsibility of instructing young soldiers in horsemanship have felt the want of an intelligent system of imparting instruction. The better horseman a man naturally is, the more difficult, as a rule, is it for him to appreciate the trouble others find in mastering what to him came as instinct; the worse he is, the more impossible will he have found it to explain to others what he has never mastered himself—and between the two stools the recruit has, often literally, found himself on the ground.

The want has not been so much felt in England with our system of regimental riding masters and rough riders, as in Germany, where every squadron leader has suffered and still suffers from it, and therefore it may be of interest to reproduce here the views of one of the finest all-round horsemen Germany has ever possessed—General von Rosenberg, who is not only a born cavalry leader and keen soldier, but who was also one of the best steeplechase riders Germany has ever produced, and would have held his own in any company in the world. As a guide to the instruction of young soldiers, his pamphlet is about the soundest and most practical I have ever come across; and as his views are widely circulated and have acquired great authority, he is now one of the inspector generals of cavalry for the German Empire—the study of them will be useful to all ranks as a key to the nature and character of the German cavalry, such as the reading of the ordinary cavalry literature can hardly give. Even the celebrated Von Schmidt's works are hardly as valuable, for though Schmidt knew what he wanted, and how to set about obtaining it, he himself was but an indifferent horseman, and thus failed to carry conviction in all he wrote.

Rosenberg begins by dividing riding into two classes—passive and active. A good "passive" rider has a grim seat, knees close to the saddle flap, light hands, and can indicate his wishes to his horse through the tension of *one rein*, or the pressure of *one leg*; he will also understand the use of the weight of his body in turning or stopping his horse, by throwing it to either side or backwards. The good "active" rider will know how, by the proper use of his weight, of his *two legs* and *both reins.*, to collect his mount and secure from it the most complete obedience. Where passive riding ceases and active riding begins it is hard to say—one can judge best by seeing the horse itself, but an example will make things clearer. A good jockey rides mostly passively till the finish begins, then he sits down, and by spur and whip brings the horse's haunches under him and secures the most extreme exertion, of the animal's powers.

> Amongst our young officers there are many excellent 'passive' riders, who sit well over jumps and are all right till the struggle comes, but then their art fails them, and they do not know what to do. The best would be to continue sitting still, but, as a rule, they do the reverse, and cutting and spurring in mimicry of the good 'active' riders, they throw their horses out of their strides, fail altogether to collect them, and ultimately reach the judge's box a good two lengths worse off than they would have done had they confined their efforts to sitting still. It is just the same in the school; a man who tries to ride 'actively' without being able really to do so, may ride 'shoulder in' and 'passage,' and from a distance appear to do it very well, but actually the horse is not properly bent or collected—in a word, it is merely 'eyewash.' To reduce an obstinate animal to obedience by punishment belongs also to 'active' horsemanship.
>
> To save a stumbling horse falls within the limitation of a 'passive' rider. To calm a violent one by quiet riding is within the scope of both; as above remarked, the exact line is difficult to be drawn, very few ever really become good 'active' riders—fortunately, it is not even necessary that they should; the average civilians or officers can get along through life very well as 'passive' riders, provided they buy either naturally quiet animals, or' such as have been thoroughly well trained by competent people. In teaching, we frequently make the mistake of demanding good 'active' riding from men we have never really taught; the ride

goes worse with every day, the men apply brute force instead of skill and tact—and who is to blame? Generally, I believe, the instructor, who is in too great a hurry and asks too much. The first thing to do is to teach the recruits good 'passive' riding; afterwards one can pick the best for further instruction.

TRAINING OF THE RECRUIT ON THE NUMNAH.

Horses turn out with *numnah* and surcingle, bridoon reins. The man first learns to sit with his weight evenly distributed between the two points of the pelvis (on which the thigh-bones are pointed), and draws the thighs as far back as he can without losing his seat on these two points. The inner surface of the thigh and the inner surface of the knee lie lightly pressed against the horse without giving the man the feeling that he is sitting on them; he must sit on his seat. The inner surface of the knee is close to the horse, without, however, squeezing him. and below the knee the legs hang free. At this stage the recruit must not even try to use the pressure of the calf. The toes at first may hang down.

For the carriage of the body nothing is to be laid down as yet, the man holds himself as may be most comfortable to him. In the trot he must let his body be thrown upwards at each step, and fall back into his original position. In the gallop, a pace which the recruit should practice at least as much as the trot, the knees, the inner surface of thighs, and the seat itself must remain close to the horse. The whole position must be free and without constraint, the small of the back drawn in, so that with each stride the rider feels a for ward thrust through the seat and the horse's back. The upper part of the trunk is used to give the rider the feeling of an easy position; generally, at first it may be allowed to lean far back with muscles quite relaxed. The reins to be held according to regulation, and the instructor must point out that they must preserve a light equal bearing on the mouth, never jerking and never pulling. A loose arm and shoulder-joint is absolutely essential to learn the proper feeling.

As soon as the recruit has acquired a little confidence after the first few days, he must jump a small obstacle at least ten times a day; to save the horses, 18 inches of height will suffice. Within six weeks—experience has shown that the time suffices—he must be able to sit over small jumps, preserving the seat above

151

indicated, and without holding on by his calves, the inner surface of the knee firmly pressed to the horse at the moment of jumping. The man must yet be taught halting and turning on the *numnah*: in the former, sitting well down on the two bones of the seat, he inclines the upper body backward and assists the horse by a slight tension of the reins. Turning is managed by inclining the weight of the body over on to the inner seat bone and a slight movement of both hands in the required direction.

The muscles of the recruit soon accustom themselves to his new work; when that much is attained, the men should ride never less than two hours daily. The longer a ride works, the more you can save the horses, and the more time can be allowed for halts and instruction. The instructor must avoid generalities. He must describe clearly and fully every feeling to each individual recruit—if necessary, show how the thing is to be done—and by questioning convince himself that he has been understood. There is no object in letting recruits fall off. It is better in the last resort to let them hold on by the mane. One must never lose patience; it only makes the men nervous, and the nervous man makes his body stiff—the very worst possible impediment to progress.

Horses should be clipped (note, recruit training in Germany is always in winter-time); not only does it save the man labour in grooming, but the clipped horse, on winter rations, can do more work than the unclipped one. The recruit who in the first six weeks rides 375 miles learns proportionately more than the one who only covers 250 miles. They must ride as much trot and gallop as the condition of the horses permits, and the gallop and jumping give the man a better feeling for the correct easy seat than the trot. The men must be encouraged by judicious praise and by exciting the feeling of emulation; they must take pleasure in riding; the man who mounts his horse with reluctance may be compelled into military forms, but he will never acquire dash and 'feeling.'

Rosenberg always used the word "feeling" to denote both hands and the correct, almost intuitive, feeling for the movements of the horse which in its highest development makes the real horseman. I can find no exact English equivalent for the word.

From the very first day the instructor must endeavour to bring a feeling of dash into his ride, and this he will do best by not destroying men's nerves by unnecessary falls. Small obstacles taken without accidents exercise a peculiar fascination on the men; they want to do more and more every day, and the best ones may be encouraged to do so, whilst the weaker ones are kept back, on the excuse that they might hurt themselves: thus one can soon induce a feeling of emulation; the recruits themselves will soon ask to be allowed to try bigger jumps, and thus by degrees the limits of the possible may be attained. All through this part of the training the knee only must be allowed to grip; the use of the calf comes later. This is a most important point, for it ensures the man's obtaining an easy seat, and only when this has been acquired can he learn to use the lower part of the leg properly. If it is not attended to, the recruit soon learns to cling with the calves, and then never becomes quite master of his limbs; and never afterwards can learn how to apply the aids correctly.

A recruit thus falsely taught on the *numnah* will take long before he can manage his stirrups; he will either cling with the calves, and then will be always losing them, or will seek in them a point of support, since he has never really acquired an easy seat, and without that knowledge he can never really learn to ride at all. This natural easy seat is the chief factor in military riding. The school rider generally sits too much on his fork, and he is quite right for his special purpose, for by so doing he can better use the lower half of the leg. Aids by balance, which can only be given in the 'easy seat' he rarely employs, for, as he does not ride across country, he does not require them; and if by chance he does get into difficult ground, he goes very gingerly and without giving his horse his head, for he has been trained always to hold his horse up by the reins, although the only true way to prevent it stumbling is by the proper use of his weight. The jockey stands in his stirrup with knees firmly pressed to the saddle, though not cramped against it, the seat above the saddle; and he, too, is right, because he spares both himself and his horse most in this manner; but this seat is useless for military riding, and generally only applicable over level ground.

The good cross-country rider sits in the same easy seat above demanded for our cavalry, and one finds it again in the good jockey when he sits down to finish. The worst possible seat is that in which the rider allows himself at every stride in the gallop to be thrown a couple of hands high in the air; neither rider nor horse can, stand it long, and every animal who possesses even the temperament of a cow will become unsteady under such a rider, and the correct execution of any evolution at a gallop becomes an impossibility.

But one finds it only too frequently in our army, and even amongst our steeplechase riders; it is entirely the consequence of false elementary training. It is much to be regretted that Seydlitz left us no hints, or so few of them, as to how the recruit was to be taught; only this much is certain, that at Trebnetz and Ohlan, where he was quartered as squadron commander and afterwards as colonel of a regiment, he had the drill-grounds and manages inclosed with barriers, so that every man had to jump to get on or off them.

I may here add that since Rosenberg wrote a good deal came to light on these points, and in Hohenlohe's conversations about cavalry it will be seen that his views must have been practically identical with Rosenberg's.

Now follows an amusing critique of a work on riding which formerly enjoyed considerable reputation in Germany. Its author's name was Von Elpons, and it must be remembered that it was his style of 'equitation under which the older cavalrymen in Germany had grown up, and against whose views Prince Frederick Charles first, and Schmidt,, Rosenberg, and others subsequently, between the years 1864 to 1876, revolted. This will explain also what I have often maintained in face of considerable opposition from the tactical authorities in England—namely, that the feats of the German cavalry in France in 1870 form no criterion of what they are capable of now in 1892, as they were then only beginning to emerge from the darkness of the old manage school. To continue, old Von Elpons remarks that many of his pupils had complained to him, "How difficult it is to understand the Prussian riding regulations!" to which he replies, "This expression, often uttered with a feeling of sad resignation, always filled me with a certain secret satisfaction."

Obviously he was of opinion that the object of instruction was not to impart light and leading, but to discriminate darkness and obscurity, a view characteristic of a certain school of instructions in military sciences in all times. Conscious of their own ignorance, their efforts have always been to avoid being found out, and they have adopted the policy of the common cuttle-fish, who exudes ink to delude his pursuers. To the end of the chapter these we shall have always with us. It is from the Elpons school that the Germans derived their tendency to an exaggerated fork seat, often so unfavourably commented on by English observers. In part, too, it is due to the shape of the Hungarian saddle, which has accreted round the original tree a mass of cushions and bolsters, comfortable for the rider, but totally useless dead weight to the horse. Against this fork seat Rosenberg is very incisive, as it utterly destroys the true balance of the upper part of the body. Next in importance to the seat comes the correct handling of the reins.

Formerly one often heard it said that the arm and shoulder-joint should remain fixed, wrist bent inwards: this practically amounts to a prohibition against moving the arm and shoulder-joint, all was to be done by a turn of the wrist alone and with the back of the hand perpendicular. It is difficult to understand how this idea, good enough in the school, came to be accepted in military riding, and quite impossible to conceive how the tradition has survived to our time; for what soldier, from the day he joins, except in a school inspection, ever dreams of adhering to the instruction literally? This turn of the wrist and its four lines of action no one understands, and, especially with the bit, no one can execute it.

When the men turn their wrists, they do so in obedience to positive orders, but the turn of movement of the horse does not follow as a consequence, but is due to other aids almost unconsciously applied. We instructors deceive the men and the men deceive us; the whole of the valuable winter-time is wasted, both horses' and men's tempers and mouths ruined, and all for an old 'humbug' (his own word), to which no one pays the slightest attention, the day after he leaves the school and his true education as a cavalryman begins. The simplest and most natural method of using the reins, one that everyone understands without difficulty, is the following:

The reins have a light, even bearing on the jaws through the bit, which always remains same; there must be no jerking still less may the horse bore against the hand; let the animal chuck his head about as he will. This entails a loose shoulder-joint and arm, which yields to every movement of the horse. Against this even pressure he will soon find it useless to fight, and will keep his head quiet; but against the attempt to keep the hand still he will soon succeed in compelling it to yield, for the horse's neck muscles are considerably stronger than those of a man's arm. The horse then finds out he can by insistence have his own way, and all the work of weeks perhaps has to be done over again.

The general is strongly of opinion that turnings are to be indicated to the horse by inclining the weight of the body inward and moving both reins in the required direction without attempting to shorten the inner one; the pressure of the outer rein on the neck is sufficient for the purpose.

Look at a squadron wheeling from the front, or at two men practicing mounted combats, and one will see that not one man in the army ever attempts to shorten the inner rein. Why, then, waste our precious time in endeavouring to teach what is of no practical value? In halting a horse, the weight of the body inclined backwards is the chief point; similarly, in saving a stumbling one, 90 *per cent* is effected by the weight, only 10 *per cent* by the reins. For this reason the custom of shortening the reins over bad ground is to be utterly condemned; not only does the horse require his head free, but if he pecks, the shortened reins drag the body forward, and before the man can recover himself the horse is down. It is a capital exercise to practice clambering up and down steep banks; it accustoms the rider to understand the distribution of his weight.

The instructor should not at first trouble about teaching a strictly military seat; this is only an outward form, only necessary in so far as uniformity of appearance is desirable as an expression of discipline. Once the man can ride, the external finish can be easily applied; but if the chief stress is laid on appearance, the result is to make wooden riders, men who fly about on their horses likes peas on a drum and job the poor animal in the mouth. With such riders no long gallop to the front, consequently no charge, can conceivably be ridden. The time spent on such things is therefore worse than wasted. The object of the training on the *numnah* is to teach a firm but easy seat, correct guidance with the reins, and balance at all paces, both in turning, jumping, and climbing, and experience shows that if this much is not attained within six to eight weeks, the instructor has mistaken his profession.

TRAINING ON THE SADDLE.

As soon as the above degree of training has been attained, recruits at once proceed to the saddle. The seat and balance remain the same, but from now the lower leg is drawn back till the calf has a light but firm bearing behind the girth. The chief difficulty is to prevent the knee-and ankle-joints becoming stiff, and to manage the stirrups, They are intended to be an aid and convenience to the man; if they are too long, he loses his seat by bending forward endeavouring to retain them; if too short, the seat is cramped by the effort to keep the calf in the proper position. The instructor must fit each man separately to suit his build. "It would be no disadvantage to let the men place the whole of the foot in the stirrup, for the easy play of the knee-joint is the chief object to keep in view, and with feet borne in the stirrup a man is safer in the ranks and over obstacles."

The man now learns to use the pressure of the calf of the leg, first on one side only, afterwards on both, but the one-sided pressure is here the chief point to which will be recurred later in the training of remounts. In galloping, the full pace of manoeuvres. 15 miles an hour (out of doors understood) and for long distances, must be practiced as much as possible, till the man is thoroughly at home in it, and the horses gallop quietly in their places without attempting to race. I may here add that the 19th Hussars are the only regiment I have ever seen in England which attained in this point the average German require-ments. It is also good at this stage to practice both the gallop and jumping without reins.

The rider thus acquires the indispensable easy seat best, and also comes to understand that over bad ground or obstacles a horse goes best with his head free. It sounds rather much to demand of the aver-age recruit, but experience shows that they soon acquire what is want-ed; and, whether or no, it is the only possible way to obtain the class of horsemen we require, for of what possible good can a cavalry be that cannot close with its enemy except over the level parade-ground type of ground that never is found in practical warfare? The men must now be taught to rise in their stirrups when trotting—this for use on the line of march and in patrolling; elsewhere, at drill, in difficult ground, generally where the horse must be unconditionally under control, the military trot can alone be used.

When the man is thoroughly at home in the saddle, and can manage his horse on the bridoon, riding on the bit and with arms is practiced. Here there is only to note that the tension of the reins is to be as light and even as possible, and the arm from the shoulder, when cutting and pointing, absolutely independent of the body. A loose shoulder joint is here the chief point.

Training of Remounts.

The main thing is to be thoroughly clear in one's own mind as to what qualifications the horse must possess to be reliable and useful in the field. The essentials are, absolute obedience and safety over all kinds of ground: by absolute obedience is understood that the horse under all conditions goes where his rider wishes, is not a puller, and obeys at once the aids applied by the leg, rein, or alteration in the balance. Safety in difficult ground is partly the result of practice, partly of the proper balance of rider and horse. Good paces may be natural, but can also be acquired under a good rider in proper balance. Proper balance being when the weight is evenly distributed over all four legs, and this is the surest means of preserving a horse from strained sinews and premature breakdown.

It is unnecessary to follow the writer through the whole of his discussion of bending lessons. Briefly, he considers the bending lesson an indispensable preliminary to acquiring unconditional obedience, but the bend, and side paces generally, must be taught by the pressure of one leg only. At this stage he will have nothing to do with the supporting pressure of the outer leg. If the horse attempts to escape by too rapid a pace, let him at first; he will soon moderate it of his own accord.

This yielding to the pressure of the leg, is a great trouble with thoroughbred horses, but it must be taught to all horses for military purposes; otherwise the rider has no power to exact obedience, and generally the animal is unfit to be ridden in the ranks. As soon as they have learnt to yield to the leg. they must next be taught "obedience." At first they will be taken quietly at a walk up to some obstacle at which it can be foreseen they will refuse to go on. The rider is on the lookout, with a light bearing of the reins, and meets the first attempt to swerve with the opposite leg. If the animal stops outright, or attempts to back, the body is inclined backwards and both legs pressed to him, till he decides to advance. Patience and endurance are the chief points, but every man in the squadron, down to the last recruit, must be able by these simple aids to compel obedience; otherwise he is useless for practical purposes.

I heard the first time of this simple method from the well-known steeplechase rider, Graf Wilamowitz, when quartered as a young officer in Breslau. At mess one night he said: 'If I want to be quite certain of a horse in a steeplechase, it must first of all refuse with me; if not, I take it out and induce it to refuse, and then compel it to obey. The animal must know that it has got to jump when I am on its back.' This made a considerable impression on me, for at the time my instructor was of the opposite opinion; he maintained that one should avoid opportunities of trying conclusions in so drastic a manner; so afterwards I took the first occasion of speaking to the Graf alone, and asked him to explain, which he kindly did. From him I learnt for the first time the meaning of light hands and the use of the lower part of the leg. It was like the flash of a distant lighthouse in a dark night and heavy sea, and I went back to my garrison feeling that I had discovered a new world. How many thousand sovereigns and how much enjoyment have I owed to that short conversation!

As already mentioned, Rosenberg soon afterwards became the most celebrated steeplechase rider in his country, and his total winnings must have run into very high figures. I first heard the idea from one of Rosenberg's old pupils, an Englishman, who had a perfect genius for winning chases. The tip has often been of value to me in ordinary circumstances, and I could not count the number of chases I have seen lost through ignorance of it; but it is worth pointing out that its correct application is impossible to a man with his knees in his mouth in the modern fashionable seat. The demands on a horse's obedience can hardly be too great, though, of course, they should be made progressively. To show to what a degree their obedience can be brought, I cite again textually:

In schools and on drill-grounds, where there are no natural obstacles, one can employ the following means: draw up a ride knee to knee, and make each horse come out, and jump a bar without wing walls; one stands behind the bar, and endeavours to frighten the horse by cracking whips, waving cloths, shooting pistols, etc. For all obstacles wing walls are to be condemned.

I asked, the other day, another pupil of Rosenberg's, whether he really had succeeded in attaining this degree of obedience, or whether his imagination and pen had not run away with him. He assured me there was no word of exaggeration in the book, and that literally every horse in the regiment would not only do all above indicated, but that Rosenberg used to drive them through paper screens and flaming wreaths of fire.

> To complete obedience, this also is necessary, that at the faster paces, particularly at a gallop, no horse leans on his bridle. (In other words, no pullers or runaways need apply.) This is only attainable when the men have a firm seat and light hand—*i. e.*, movable arm and loose shoulder-joint. If such animals are met with, then give them to the best and strongest riders to gallop them 'bent'—*i. e.,* placed as for 'shoulder in' for considerable distances. This procedure is also recommended to anyone who has the misfortune to come in for a hard-mouthed horse ruined on the race-course—a bolter, in fact.

It must be confessed, to pass a satisfactory inspection before Rosenberg must be no child's play, and I wonder how many of our own squadrons would survive the ordeal with credit. Yet if the Germans, with three years' service, can accomplish it, surely the matter is within our power. Against our bigger and somewhat more intemperate horses (in size, by the way, their *cuirassiers* and Uhlans are at least equal to ours) we may safely set our seven years' service and the undeniable superiority of our men in natural taste for horsemanship. To continue—when the horses have learnt to go with their heads steady, without tossing, and a light feeling on the mouth, and, further, understand the pressure of the leg on one side only, one can proceed to collect their quarters under them by the pressure of both legs, to bring about the even distribution of weight on all four legs above referred to, and for this purpose the practice of a short collected trot is the best means, when the eye of the instructor is the best guide as to whether the quarters really are brought under the body or not.

Then follows the collected canter. Again, the object is not the shortness of the stride, but the degree to which the quarters arc really brought under. This must be proceeded with very gradually; it cannot be hurried without the risk of breaking down the animal or ruining its temper. Its object is, besides making the horse more obedient, to strengthen the back muscles so as to give it greater speed and endurance when really extended. It is an utter mistake to imagine, as many do, that this collected canter, if properly acquired, cramps a horse's stride: exactly the contrary is the case. The ideal gallop for speed is seen best in the greyhound, and the nearer the race-horse can approximate to the type the better; but in the greyhound the unaided eye can see distinctly the back arched and the quarters tucked under, and it is the same power of arching the back that one seeks' to acquire by the collected canter. It is simply a kind of gymnastic exercise. Hundreds of horses race without really possessing it; they wobble their legs like compasses from the point of the shoulder and thigh- joint, with considerable celerity certainly, but they do not eat up the ground.

As regards training the young horse to jump, he approves of driving them unbacked down a lane with obstacles, the height of which is gradually increased. Then the lane must be widened from 10 to 15 paces, and the horses ridden. Except to teach obedience, he is entirely against jumping from the trot or walk, as it is unnatural to the horse. He has no objection to their rushing their fences somewhat, provided they do not stop short and back over. It may in peacetime spoil the dressing of a line; in war-time condition, the rushing will correct itself. A wide jump of 8 to 9 feet suffices; and once the horses jump fairly willingly, they must be trained over jumps without wing walls. On climbing up and down steep banks he lays particular importance.

The headings, on position of the head and bending lessons, are too long and too technical for translation. For the former he agrees with our drill-book, neck bent only at the poll, and face between the perpendicular and 45 degrees—just, in fact, where the horse naturally carries it against a light hand. Bending beyond the amount necessary to secure obedience he considers unnecessary for military purposes, and would gladly see it cut out of the book altogether. The chapter on race-riding and hunting is quite excellent;, only, unfortunately, my space begins to fail me. One or two points deserve attention. Rosenberg is most bitter against those cavalrymen in his country who believe that the school and drill-ground suffice for the training of officers and men, and recalls the many sins of omission to the discredit of the arm in Bohemia and France.

On the other hand, he is quite as merciless on those of his comrades who think because they can ride a steeplechase or follow the hounds without falling off, therefore they have nothing to learn from military equitation. Both are essential to perfection in either, and he is particularly down on the theory that correct training and balance injures a horse's speed, but to that I have already referred above. The tactical part must form material for another chapter. In conclusion, I would beg those who have followed me thus far to remember that these are the views of no theoretical horseman, but of one of the first cavalrymen in Europe, and everything he says is founded on years of experience. If, therefore, some of his demands appear excessive and not attainable from our cavalry as it is, the fault must be in our system of training—or, rather, in the way in which the system is interpreted.

We have made immense progress in the past few years, which should enourage us to further efforts; but, judging by the printed reports of last year's cavalry manoeuvres, the tendency seems to be to assume that our individual horsemanship and squadron leading is all that can be desired, and failures are to be attributed to the tactical employment of the arm, and not to the deficiencies within the squadrons themselves. The endeavour to disinter the corrupt old theory of a charge in many echelons, instead of with the bulk of force in line, is a case in point. If we cannot charge sixteen squadrons in line, it is not because the thing is in itself impossible, but simply because our individual training and squadron leading is not up to the required standard. Squadrons that attain Rosenberg's standard can be handled by sixties even, and no one can maintain that the individual men or squadrons trained to satisfy his conditions would be less useful in minor operations than our own.

The charge in many echelons broke down years ago, because the practical difficulty of keeping the true direction in each echelon was too great, and because the two or three squadrons in the single echelon neither conveyed to the men themselves nor to the enemy the same impression of irresistible force as did the line of sixteen or more. Besides, with men properly trained and horses properly broken, the flanks of the long line were not so defenceless as is imagined, for, up to the moment the "charge" is sounded, the flank squadrons can wheel up to meet a threatened attack. The refused flank in the formation in many echelons might be somewhat the safer, but the other was in even greater danger than the long line; for, if the outer squadron was attacked and ridden over, the debris drifted across the front of the second and third, whereas, if the flank of the long line is attacked and overthrown, the rest of the line has swept clear before any trouble can arise.

The outer squadron wheeling up and the second line echeloned in rear in the ordinary formation should be quite sufficient to safeguard the flank. Besides the difficulty of maintaining the direction in an advance in several echelons, there is the difficulty of the distances to be covered by each at a gallop. The formation must be completed at some distance from the enemy, and if we take 600 yards as this distance, and twenty squadrons in five echelons of four squadrons apiece at 100 yards' distance, then the refused flank has 1,000 yards in all to traverse, and the extra 400 yards will make all the difference in the condition of the horses at the moment of impact.

As the leading echelon nears the enemy the pace is gradually increased, the next echelon, to keep distance, increases its pace, too, and so on along the whole line, so that the fifth will probably have to cover some 400 additional yards almost at charging pace before it closes with the enemy. There is nothing new under the sun, and this old echelon attack has been trotted out again and again in peacetime, always to succumb in time of war, and the existing charge with the bulk of the force in first line has as invariably succeeded. Past experience, therefore, seems to me reason enough for retaining it.

LEONAUR

ALSO FROM LEONAUR
AVAILABLE IN SOFTCOVER OR HARDCOVER WITH DUST JACKET

THE ART OF WAR *by Antoine Henri Jomini*—Strategy & Tactics From the Age of Horse & Musket.

THE ART OF WAR *by Sun Tzu and Pierre G. T. Beauregard*—*The Art of War* by Sun Tzu and *Principles and Maxims of the Art of War* by Pierre G.T. Beauregard.

THE MILITARY RELIGIOUS ORDERS OF THE MIDDLE AGES *by F. C. Woodhouse*—The Knights Templar, Hospitaller and Others.

THE BENGAL NATIVE ARMY *by F. G. Cardew*—An Invaluable Reference Resource.

ARTILLERY THROUGH THE AGES—*by Albert Manucy*—A History of the DEvelopment and Use of Cannons, Mortars, Rockets & Projectiles from Earliest Times to the Nineteenth Century.

THE SWORD OF THE CROWN *by Eric W. Sheppard*—A History of the British Army to 1914.

THE 7TH (QUEEN'S OWN) HUSSARS: Volume 3—1818-1914 *by C. R. B. Barrett*—On Campaign During the Canadian Rebellion, the Indian Mutiny, the Sudan, Matabeleland, Mashonaland and the Boer War Volume 3: 1818-1914.

THE CAMPAIGN OF WATERLOO *by Antoine Henri Jomini*—A Political & Military History from the French perspective.

RIFLE & DRILL *by S. Bertram Browne*—The Enfield Rifle Musket, 1853 and the Drill of the British Soldier of the Mid-Victorian Period *A Companion to the New Rifle Musket* and *A Practical Guide to Squad and Setting-up Dtill.*

NAPOLEON'S MEN AND METHODS *by Alexander L. Kielland*—The Rise and Fall of the Emperor and His Men Who Fought by His Side.

THE WOMAN IN BATTLE *by Loreta Janeta Velazquez*—Soldier, Spy and Secret Service Agent for the Confederancy During the American Civil War.

THE BATTLE OF ORISKANY 1777 *by Ellis H. Roberts*—The Conflict for the Mowhawk Valley During the American War of Independenc.

PERSONAL RECOLLECTIONS OF JOAN OF ARC *by Mark Twain.*

CAESAR'S ARMY *by Harry Pratt Judson*—The Evolution, Composition, Tactics, Equipment & Battles of the Roman Army.

FREDERICK THE GREAT & THE SEVEN YEARS' WAR *by F. W. Longman.*

LEONAUR

ALSO FROM LEONAUR
AVAILABLE IN SOFTCOVER OR HARDCOVER WITH DUST JACKET

OFFICERS & GENTLEMEN by Peter Hawker & William Graham—Two Accounts of British Officers During the Peninsula War: Officer of Light Dragoons by Peter Hawker & Campaign in Portugal and Spain by William Graham .

THE WALCHEREN EXPEDITION by Anonymous—The Experiences of a British Officer of the 81st Regt. During the Campaign in the Low Countries of 1809.

LADIES OF WATERLOO by Charlotte A. Eaton, Magdalene de Lancey & Juana Smith—The Experiences of Three Women During the Campaign of 1815: Waterloo Days by Charlotte A. Eaton, A Week at Waterloo by Magdalene de Lancey & Juana's Story by Juana Smith.

JOURNAL OF AN OFFICER IN THE KING'S GERMAN LEGION by John Frederick Hering—Recollections of Campaigning During the Napoleonic Wars.

JOURNAL OF AN ARMY SURGEON IN THE PENINSULAR WAR by Charles Boutflower—The Recollections of a British Army Medical Man on Campaign During the Napoleonic Wars.

ON CAMPAIGN WITH MOORE AND WELLINGTON by Anthony Hamilton—The Experiences of a Soldier of the 43rd Regiment During the Peninsular War.

THE ROAD TO AUSTERLITZ by R. G. Burton—Napoleon's Campaign of 1805.

SOLDIERS OF NAPOLEON by A. J. Doisy De Villargennes & Arthur Chuquet—The Experiences of the Men of the French First Empire: Under the Eagles by A. J. Doisy De Villargennes & Voices of 1812 by Arthur Chuquet .

INVASION OF FRANCE, 1814 by F. W. O. Maycock—The Final Battles of the Napoleonic First Empire.

LEIPZIG—A CONFLICT OF TITANS by Frederic Shoberl—A Personal Experience of the 'Battle of the Nations' During the Napoleonic Wars, October 14th-19th, 1813.

SLASHERS by Charles Cadell—The Campaigns of the 28th Regiment of Foot During the Napoleonic Wars by a Serving Officer.

BATTLE IMPERIAL by Charles William Vane—The Campaigns in Germany & France for the Defeat of Napoleon 1813-1814.

SWIFT & BOLD by Gibbes Rigaud—The 60th Rifles During the Peninsula War.